FBI HEROES

Allan Zullo

SCHOLASTIC INC.

To my grandson Chad Manausa, with the hope that he will always take to heart the motto of the FBI: "Fidelity, Bravery, and Integrity."

—A.Z.

ISBN 978-0-545-46040-8

12 11 10 9 8 7 6 5 4 3 2 1   13 14 15 16 17 18/0

Printed in the U.S.A.   40
First edition, October 2013

ACKNOWLEDGMENTS

I wish to thank all the special agents in this book for their willingness to recall details, in personal interviews with me, of specific cases — even when they were crammed for time at work.

This book could not have been done without the full cooperation of the FBI, especially of Public Affairs Specialist Angela Bell in the FBI Office of Public Affairs in Washington, D.C. She was instrumental in helping me select cases and in paving the way for my interviews. For all of Ms. Bell's efforts, I am extremely grateful.

My appreciation extends to those field-office media coordinators who set up interviews and provided me with additional information: Special Agent Shauna Dunlap, Houston Division; Special Agent Frank Burton Jr., Philadelphia Division; Public Affairs Specialist Katherine Chaumont, Dallas Division; Public Affairs Specialist Lindsay Godwin, Washington, D.C., Division; Public Affairs Specialist Beth Anne Steele, Portland (Oregon) Division; Public Affairs Specialist Jim Marshall, Miami Division; Special Agent Stephen Emmett, Atlanta Division; Special Agent Dave Couvertier, Tampa Division; Special Agent Jacqueline Maguire, Washington, D.C., Division; and Public Affairs Specialists Susan McKee and Debbie Weierman of the FBI Office of Public Affairs.

CONTENTS

THE BUREAU

E ver since it was formed more than 100 years ago, the Federal Bureau of Investigation (FBI) has defended and protected our country from countless threats to our way of life, and has brought hardened criminals to justice.

Today, the main mission of the FBI is to guard the United States from terrorist and foreign intelligence threats, enforce the country's criminal laws, and assist other law-enforcement agencies.

Over the decades, the FBI has captured murderers, terrorists, and spies; rescued kidnap victims, hostages, and captives; dismantled street gangs, drug cartels, and organized crime families; uncovered public corruption, white-collar scams, and criminal conspiracies; solved hate crimes, violent crimes, and high-tech crimes; prevented terrorist acts, cyber attacks, and domestic bombings; busted bank robbery rings, burglary rings, and smuggling rings; nabbed violent ecoterrorists, antigovernment extremists, and white supremacists; battled against identity theft, Internet fraud, and counterfeit schemes; and thwarted illegal arms dealers, human traffickers, and child predators.

The Bureau solves cases and prevents crimes through the dedicated efforts of more than 36,000 employees. The force includes nearly 14,000 special agents and more than 22,000 support professionals, such as laboratory technicians, intelligence analysts, scientists, forensics specialists, bomb experts, behavioral analysts, and information technology specialists.

This book features ten compelling stories about special agents who cracked difficult cases — from mass murder on the high seas to the kidnapping of a newborn baby, from the theft of priceless moon rocks to the capture of the country's most elusive bank robber. In lengthy personal interviews, these agents recalled their sometimes frustrating but ultimately successful investigations that led to the arrest and conviction of dangerous criminals. The stories, which are supported by court documents and law enforcement records, were written from the point of view of the chief investigators as they collected clues and followed leads until the cases were solved.

All the agents profiled in this book shared a common trait — humility. None took sole credit for bringing the perpetrators to justice. Each agent stressed that it was a team effort, that he or she worked together with fellow agents and members of other law-enforcement agencies. In addition, the agents emphasized that they utilized the FBI's vast resources, including the technological know-how of its support professionals, to solve these challenging cases.

Once you begin reading the stories in this book, you will understand why these remarkable men and women live up to the Bureau's motto: "Fidelity, Bravery, and Integrity."

THE CASE OF THE DALLAS TERRORIST

Alone terrorist plotting to unleash a weapon of mass destruction was freely walking the streets, unaware that his every move was being monitored 24/7 by the FBI.

Supervisory Special Agent Tom Petrowski and his team were enduring many sleepless nights during this top secret undercover operation. They understood that if they botched the case or if the terrorist discovered they were onto him, the consequences would be disastrous: the senseless slaughter of hundreds of innocent people.

Petrowski, an agent with the Bureau since 1995, was managing the operation out of the FBI's field office in Dallas, Texas, where he supervised the Counterterrorism-2 squad (CT-2). Like all FBI agents, Petrowski and his team found it disturbing that there are so many websites promoting

1

bloodthirsty jihad — acts of terrorism in the name of Islam. Radicals, many using fake names, spew their loathing for the United States in online chat groups, endorsing and celebrating acts of terrorism against American citizens, soldiers, and allies. Rather than muster holy armies of warriors, terrorist groups are resorting to a different weapon of choice — the angry loner who is emotionally connected with the jihadist philosophy. He's so easily influenced by hate-filled propaganda on the Internet that he's willing to carry out acts of death and devastation on his own free will.

One such violence-prone lone wolf was the focus of CT-2's undercover operation: 19-year-old Hosam "Sam" Smadi.

In January 2009, an Arab-speaking undercover FBI agent posing as an extremist on an online forum of Islamic radicals noticed that someone named Abu al Ayyubi seemed different from the others. While many praised violence, al Ayyubi stood out because he said he yearned to be a soldier for Osama bin Laden, who was, at the time, the leader of al-Qaeda, the terrorist organization responsible for the 9/11 attacks in 2001. Pledging his allegiance to al-Qaeda, al Ayyubi said he was already in the U.S. and hoped to carry out terrorism here, but needed help. "I can strike at their interests in their midst," he wrote in the online forum. "The targets are easy."

The FBI discovered that al Ayyubi was really Hosam Smadi. A background check showed he was born in the

Middle Eastern country of Jordan and came to the U.S. on March 14, 2007, at the age of 16 on a temporary visa, which expired on October 30 of that year. He was living about an hour's drive south of Dallas, where he worked in a restaurant off Interstate 35.

After several email exchanges with Smadi, the undercover extremist introduced him online to Rafiq, a second Arab-speaking undercover agent, in early 2009. Acting as a senior al-Qaeda leader who assessed new recruits, Rafiq cultivated a relationship with Smadi over the next several months. The two engaged in two dozen online conversations about Smadi's desire to commit a major terrorist attack.

In one such message to Rafiq on March 19, Smadi wrote, "I truly say it, that my dream is to be among God's soldiers, first for the support of Islam and my beloved Sheik Osama, may God give him long life. I don't know what is in me, but I love him as I love my father. . . . In the name of God, the Gracious and Merciful, this is my vow to you, my brother, that I am ready . . . for the Jihadi life. What you will see of me will please you and your Commander."

Ten days later, Smadi emailed Rafiq again, "We shall attack them in their very homes. Brother, by God, we shall attack them in a manner that hurts, an attack that shakes the world. Oh Brother, let the backsliders know that the time of their destruction has come."

No matter how many times Rafiq suggested nonviolent forms of jihad, Smadi remained steadfast in wanting to strike against America. In an email on April 7, he declared, "I have chosen to be a *Mujahidin* [an Islamic guerrilla fighter] with my self, blood, soul, and body. [That is] more precious to me than this world and its money, women, and amusements."

Petrowski and his team still harbored doubts that Smadi really intended to carry out a terrorist act. After all, talk is cheap. To get a better understanding of him, the FBI arranged, through Rafiq, for Smadi to meet a third Arabic-speaking undercover agent in person. The agent posed as Brother Hussein, a member of an al-Qaeda sleeper cell (a secret group of terrorists in the United States). Even though there was no actual sleeper cell, Hussein acted as one of its low-level operational soldiers who was there to assist Smadi. As part of his cover, Hussein said he had been in the U.S. for several years and was a businessman in the Southeast.

The first time the two met face-to-face, Smadi told Hussein, "When I came to this country, I came for the purpose which is jihad."

After the meeting, the undercover agent told the CT-2 team, "I have an overwhelming feeling this guy is for real. My initial assessment is that he's serious about committing a terrorist attack."

Petrowski brought in experts from the FBI's Behavioral Analysis Unit (BAU) to help determine how great a threat Smadi posed. Every communication that undercover agents had with Smadi had been electronically recorded. In face-to-face meetings with Smadi, Hussein wore a hidden microphone while other agents who were out of sight took photos and video. After reviewing and analyzing the transcripts of those conversations, senior agents and BAU experts trained in conducting psychological profiles of criminals came to the same conclusion: Smadi was a lone extremist obsessed with bin Laden and had an unwavering desire to commit a major act of terrorism in the Dallas area.

Smadi was now considered a legitimate threat.

FBI intelligence analyst Sheeren Zaidi studied Smadi's communications to peel back his inner personality and find the deep-seated reasons that powered his motivation. She concluded that for the first time in his life, Smadi felt important because he believed he was working for al-Qaeda.

Investigations conducted by senior agents and task-force officers, including Detective Mitch Bird of the Dallas Police Department, helped the team chart Smadi's transformation from a likeable Jordanian kid into a seething radical. Smadi grew up in northern Jordan with a brother and sister. He had many Christian friends, and even attended chapel at a nearby Baptist school, where he was a student. His strict father, who was a government employee, and his loving mother were both strong supporters of Jordan's pro-American royal family. Smadi's life flipped upside down after his parents divorced and then his mother died of cancer in 2005 when he was 15. Angry at the world, he began embracing jihad.

THE CASE OF THE DALLAS TERRORIST

Smadi developed a smoldering hatred for America because of what he perceived to be anti-Muslim foreign policies of the United States, Jordan, and neighboring Egypt.

Around this time, he and his brother dropped out of school, so their father obtained visas and sent them to live with relatives in San Jose, California, in 2007. After his visa expired seven months later, Smadi, who spoke English, remained in the U.S. on his own. He moved to Italy, Texas, where a friend got him a job at the Texas Best Smokehouse as a cashier, stock boy, and clerk. Known as Sam to his new pals, Smadi lived in a housing complex of individual domed structures. He wore earrings, liked techno music, partied, smoked, and drank alcohol — behavior frowned upon by observant Muslims. He rarely prayed and never fasted during the holy month of Ramadan, which are religious requirements of adult Muslims. He seldom spent time with his relatives in the Dallas area, nor did he talk much to his friends about politics, terrorism, or the Middle East. The short, slightly built young man dressed and acted like a typical Texas teenager and was often seen wearing a belt buckle decorated with rhinestones in the shape of a gun. What none of his American friends knew was that he spent hours alone on the Internet preparing for jihad against their country.

The FBI could have deported Smadi because he was living in the U.S. illegally. But the Bureau believed that if he were returned to the Middle East, he would join a terrorist group as a prized recruit. With a false identity, he likely would try to sneak back into the country to launch a terrorist attack.

Thinking it was safer to keep him under the watchful eye of agents, the highest levels of the FBI in Washington, D.C., ordered a complex sting operation run by Petrowski and his core team of CT-2 investigators — Agents David Marshall, Michael Howell, Michael Decker, Robert Benton, and Kevin Gentry — and Detective Bird. In a strictly controlled manner, the team would continue to work closely with undercover Agents Rafiq and Hussein. For the sting to succeed legally, all the ideas and research for Smadi's terrorist scheme had to come directly from him. The job of the undercover agents was to help, or pretend to help, him toward his sinister goal — up to a point. Then, when the time was right, the FBI would arrest and prosecute Smadi.

The strategy meant that Smadi could continue to walk freely while he plotted his big day of murder and mayhem. It also meant that the CT-2 squad had to make certain that he would never, ever get the opportunity to actually carry it out.

Analysts told Petrowski that because of Smadi's anti-American feelings and his belief that he was now a member of an al-Qaeda sleeper cell, it was unlikely he would act spontaneously or recklessly. But that was only if the FBI kept the investigation secret from him.

"What would happen if Smadi found out his sleeper cell is a sting operation?" Petrowski asked a BAU profiler.

THE CASE OF THE DALLAS TERRORIST

The profiler replied, "If he finds out that your guys are FBI, he likely will do something very violent, very quickly."

And that's why everyone on the CT-2 squad was having sleepless nights. There could be no mistakes, no miscalculations, no misunderstandings.

The Bureau's Counterterrorism Division in Washington began tracking the team's efforts daily and provided briefings to FBI Director Robert Mueller and even, at times, to the president of the United States.

Agents put Smadi under constant surveillance, but it wasn't easy. Because he lived in a rural area, there were times when they couldn't just tail him in a car or mill around the restaurant without being obvious. So, with the help of its tech agents, the FBI tracked his cell phone and his car and continued to monitor his emails and phone calls. As a precaution, his name was put on a terrorist watch list, which would prevent him from trying to leave the country.

Over the next few months, the physical surveillance unit noticed he was changing his appearance. As he grew to consider himself a soldier of al-Qaeda, he dressed a little flashier and sported more facial hair.

On several occasions, Smadi told Rafiq and Hussein he wasn't a practicing Muslim and didn't go to mosque. He said his relatives in the Dallas area and the local Islamic community didn't share his extremist, violent views of jihad. "They just don't get it," he complained.

THE CASE OF THE DALLAS TERRORIST

After Rafiq and Hussein gained his trust, Smadi told them it felt wonderful to share his real self with them and not be the fake person that he was to everyone else.

Despite ongoing efforts by the undercover agents to talk Smadi out of the operation, he plowed forward with unrelenting determination. The harder they pushed, the more passionate he was in committing jihad. During a meeting with Hussein at a Dallas hotel on May 12, Smadi made his intentions perfectly clear: "I want to destroy . . . targets . . . Everything that helps America on its war on Arabs will be targeted."

Throughout the spring, Smadi researched types of bombs and scouted possible sites in the Dallas area for a terrorist attack. On July 16, Smadi had settled on a target — Fountain Place, a gleaming 62-story office building in the heart of the Dallas business district. With a twisting blue-green glass exterior, the building has been one of the most recognizable structures in the city's skyline. It got its name because it rose from a tree-lined water garden featuring 172 dancing fountains, waterfalls, and pools. Among its tenants at the time were government agencies and banks, including the Wells Fargo bank.

"God willing, the strike will be certain and strong," Smadi emailed Rafiq. "It will shake the currently weak economy in the state and the American nation because this bank is one of the largest banks in the city. . . .

THE CASE OF THE DALLAS TERRORIST

". . . The bank has billions of dollars. Let's say that the bank has collapsed . . . The losses will be excessive in credit-card information. Millions of people would incur losses: unemployment, poverty, hunger, and a strike to the head of the government. Don't forget the psychological impacts for the loss of this beautiful building."

Five days later, Hussein traveled to Italy, Texas, and picked up Smadi, who directed him to drive to the Wells Fargo bank at Fountain Place. Hussein dropped him off so Smadi could conduct his own reconnaissance of the building. When Smadi returned, he said that he had found a good place to plant a bomb that would "rock the foundation."

During their fourth meeting together at a Dallas hotel, Hussein mentioned that the sleeper cell could forward a video message from Smadi to bin Laden before the bombing. Given the opportunity to address his hero, Smadi became emotionally overwhelmed. To prepare a statement for this meaningful occasion, he spent hours on his laptop researching passages from the Koran, the sacred text of Islam.

In a hotel room that was bugged with recording devices, Hussein set up a tripod and video camera for Smadi. The terrorist had no clue that members of the CT-2 squad were watching everything on a monitor in the next room. An Arabic-speaking interpreter was by their side to give them a real-time translation.

THE CASE OF THE DALLAS TERRORIST

Wearing a red-and-white-checked head covering that hid everything but his blazing eyes, Smadi made an impassioned seven-minute video for bin Laden. He told his idol that Allah had allowed "for me to join your organization from inside the enemy's midst." Of the impending bombing, Smadi said, "I hope that you are delighted by what you see, and the greatest joy will be after the success of the operation." A minute later, he wagged his finger and declared, "The date of the blessed strikes, September 11, was a celebration for us. So let us make another date a celebration for us that history will mark." Referring to all-out conflict in the U.S., Smadi said, "I cannot wait to be with you in this war on the same land, Allah willing."

Watching him on the monitor, Petrowski and the agents felt chilled by his ardent devotion to bin Laden. "It's amazing that someone can be that committed to evil for no apparent, rational reason," Petrowski told his team. "I had served in the Middle East for the military and for the Bureau and had come face-to-face with people like him. But that was a world away, not in a hotel in a city where we and our families live."

A month later, on August 26, Smadi met with Hussein for the fifth time and discussed plans for bombing Fountain Place. He wanted the sleeper cell to make him an explosive device that would collapse the entire building. He insisted the bomb have a complicated arming system and be detonated by cell phone. According to his plan, he would transport the bomb in a truck that he would park in Fountain

Place's underground garage. Once he was a safe distance away, he alone would enter the numbers on the cell phone to set off the bomb.

Agents Howell and Marshall asked the bomb lab at FBI headquarters in Quantico, Virginia, and bomb technicians in Dallas, Texas, to build a bomb that met Smadi's specifications. The technicians created an explosive device that looked real in every way — except it wouldn't actually blow up. The fake bomb included a timer, 550 pounds of explosive-grade ammonium nitrate fertilizer, and inert (meaning inactive) blasting caps placed within inert C-4 explosive blocks. All the elements of the bomb were packed inside a series of large rubber storage containers linked together with wires.

On September 18, Rafiq replied in an email to Smadi's question about when the attack should take place: "This holiday celebration that you prepared for along with Brother Hussein shall occur on Thursday, the twenty-fourth of this current month. Brother Hussein will bring to you the gift that you requested him to prepare."

The gift was a black 2001 Ford Explorer Sport Trac packed with the fake explosives.

Two days after the email, Smadi wrote back, "Let the drums of victory be struck in our holiday. We know that Allah is with us. We ask Him to bless our gift with His angels protecting and assisting us. On this day I tell you that I am ready to receive the gift. Thank you . . . May this be only the beginning, and what is coming will be greater."

THE CASE OF THE DALLAS TERRORIST

The day before the planned attack, Smadi moved out of his residence and into an isolated mobile home that he intended to use as a hideout. Agents Marshall and Howell, leaders of the five-man takedown team that would arrest the terrorist, were methodically going over their checklists.

On September 24, the day that Smadi imagined would bring him jihadist glory, the CT-2 team got into position to execute the final phase of the sting.

With FBI agents, police, cameras, and listening devices watching and recording his every move, Smadi met Hussein on the top outdoor deck of the West End Parking Center several blocks from Fountain Place. In honor of this highly anticipated day, Smadi was dressed from head to toe in black — with a bright red tie. He even wore a black cowboy hat.

"Let's go get a smoke, say a prayer, relax, and take some time," Hussein suggested.

Smadi shook his head. "No, we're doing this right now."

Hussein then gave Smadi the keys to the bomb-laden vehicle. Inside was a list of instructions on how to activate the bomb and use the cell phone to trigger the blast. After inspecting the explosives that were crammed in the back and in the covered bed of the vehicle, Smadi hopped in and drove alone toward Fountain Place.

Petrowski was in a parked car along the terrorist's route. As Smadi drove past, the agent got a good look at him and was struck by how intense he appeared. Smadi was leaning so far forward that his chin was almost touching the steering wheel, and his face was contorted into a cold stare that alarmed the veteran agent. Instantly vanishing in Petrowski's mind was any lingering doubts that Smadi would chicken out. This young jihadist was all in.

Smadi drove the vehicle into the underground garage at Fountain Place and parked in a spot reserved for bank customers. Then he followed the detailed instructions to arm the bomb. After he set it, he got out of the Explorer, locked it, and walked across the street during the busy lunch hour.

Hussein picked him up and drove back to the top of the West End parking deck so they could watch the death and destruction from a safe vantage point. As they stepped outside, Hussein offered Smadi earplugs, but the terrorist declined, saying he wanted to hear the full effects of the blast. Smadi then snapped a picture of the building he thought he was about to destroy.

Hunkered in a stairwell about 20 yards away were Howell, Marshall, Bird, and the rest of the takedown team, all clad in bulletproof vests. Although they couldn't see anything outside because they were hiding, they had been following Smadi's movements by listening to radio transmissions from the surveillance units. The team knew exactly where Smadi was on the parking deck because Hussein had delivered him to a prearranged spot near the doorway to the stairs. No one said a word. All were ready to spring into action once the signal was given.

Outside, Smadi dialed the cell phone number that he believed would trigger the explosion. The number, however, didn't blow up the building. Instead it lit the cell phone in Howell's hand. The agent held it up for the rest of the takedown team to see. Flashing for just an instant in the minds of the agents were the haunting 9/11 images of the collapsing World Trade Center towers.

Cursing in Arabic because Fountain Place was still standing, Smadi dialed the number again. He was totally oblivious to the takedown team that quietly charged out of the stairwell behind him. "FBI! You're under arrest!" Howell announced. Agents shoved Smadi to the ground, pinned his arms and legs, handcuffed him, and lifted him to his feet. Meanwhile, another agent hustled Hussein away. It was all over in a few seconds.

The moment he heard that Smadi had been arrested, Petrowski had mixed feelings. He was incredibly proud that members of his team, who had put their hearts and souls into this operation for nine months, had done such a magnificent job. *Thank goodness we found him before any terrorist organization did*, the agent told himself. And then he was struck with a disturbing thought: *How many more Hosam Smadis are out there that we don't know about?*

Immediately after Smadi's arrest, Howell and Marshall questioned him for several hours. The agents had spent more time preparing for this interview — about two months — than for any other in their careers, so they were fully versed in his emails and conversations with the undercover agents.

Smadi kept trying to minimize his crime, claiming he never actually carried out any act of terrorism. When he learned that the FBI had been keeping an eye on him for nine months, he asked Howell, "Why didn't you stop me for, like, everything?"

The agent replied, "You had the free will to stop doing this at any time, and you chose to go all the way through and plant the bomb."

Later in the interview, Howell told Smadi, "And time and time again, in every email, in every phone call, in every face-to-face meeting, and then today, you chose to do the wrong thing. That's over one hundred times."

By the end of the four-hour interrogation, Smadi was deflated and defeated.

"After Smadi's arrest, there was a lot of chatter on jihadist websites around the world," Petrowski recalled. "As for retaliation, all of our names and faces got out there. Yeah, it was a concern. But it was part of the job."

The agent said his team was helped by local police, the multiagency Joint Terrorism Task Force (JTTF), attorneys in the U.S. Department of Justice, and the FBI Counterterrorism Division in Washington.

In May 2010, Smadi pleaded guilty to one count of attempted use of a weapon of mass destruction. Five months later, he was sentenced to 24 years in prison. After serving *his time, he will be deported to Jordan just like his brother was shortly after the arrest.*

During his sentencing, Smadi, who was dressed in an orange prison jumpsuit, told the court, "I am so ashamed for what I did. I am guilty of this ugly, evil crime that targeted innocent people — women and children . . . I am very sorry for my action . . . Osama bin Laden is a bad man. I hate al-Qaeda."

U.S. District Court Judge Barbara Lynn was unmoved. "Every day from this day forward, Mr. Smadi, I want you to think of the people in that building," she told him. "They are completely innocent people whose lives you were prepared to end. For what? You were about to commit one of the great travesties and injustices of our time. That is a burden you will have to carry."

THE CASE OF THE BABY YAIR KIDNAPPING

Time was of the essence for special agents Andrea Ahumada and Eric Brown. They were trying to help find and rescue a four-day-old infant who had been snatched from his mother by a stranger.

Acting quickly is critical because many abducted children are murdered within a few hours of being kidnapped. So there was a tremendous sense of urgency when the agents joined the Metropolitan Nashville Police Department and Tennessee Bureau of Investigation (TBI) in the case of baby Yair Carrillo. A command post was set up at the TBI's Tennessee Fusion Center, where agents launched an around-the-clock effort to return the baby to his mother and nab the kidnapper.

It all began on Tuesday afternoon, September 29, 2009.

THE CASE OF THE BABY YAIR KIDNAPPING

Thirty-year-old Mexican immigrant Maria Gurrola was cuddling her infant son in their modest home in Nashville. The baby, dressed in a blue-and-white-striped onesie, was sound asleep in her arms. Maria's three-year-old daughter, Estrella, was playing on the floor while two other children, sons Orlando, eleven, and Cristian, nine, were in elementary school, and her husband, Jose Antonio Carrillo, was at work.

Hearing a knock on the front door, Maria left the baby on the couch and went to see who was there. It was an overweight woman who said she was an immigration agent. The woman accused Maria of giving false information to officials at a health center that Maria had visited earlier that morning. After Maria denied the accusation, the woman went to her car and returned with several plastic zip ties looped together — the kind that federal officials sometimes use as handcuffs. The woman then demanded that Maria hand over the baby. When Maria refused, the woman rushed into the kitchen, grabbed a butcher knife that was lying by the stove, and stabbed the mother in the head, neck, chest, and thigh. Bleeding and in shock, Maria staggered out of the house to a neighbor's seeking help. When the neighbor ran back to Maria's house, the stranger and the baby were gone. Fortunately, Maria's daughter was unharmed.

After learning of the crime, Ahumada and Brown, who were classmates at the FBI National Academy two years earlier, shared the same thought: They feared for the baby's life.

THE CASE OF THE BABY YAIR KIDNAPPING

We can't afford to waste a second, Ahumada thought. She went immediately to the victim's house, where a blue sign heralding "It's a Boy!" stood in the front yard behind yellow crime-scene tape that surrounded the residence. Inside, an Evidence Response Team analyst was looking for clues.

Ahumada then went to the Vanderbilt University Medical Center, where Maria was being treated for eight stab wounds. The victim said that the kidnapper was a white woman in her thirties, about five feet four inches tall, and heavyset. The suspect's blond hair was pulled back into a ponytail. She was wearing a black blouse and blue jeans. And she was driving a dark blue four-door sedan that Maria said looked like a police car.

The victim was distraught and in pain as she answered Ahumada's questions about the attack. Did she know or recognize the kidnapper? Were there any persons who had conflicts with her or her family? Were there any people who had displayed an unusual interest in the baby? Had she seen anything odd in the neighborhood, such as unfamiliar cars or strangers? Maria kept shaking her head no.

It seems like a random attack, Ahumada thought. *I can't figure out why she had been targeted.*

"Please, please get my baby back," Maria pleaded.

"I assure you we will do everything possible to find your baby and return him safely," replied Ahumada, who spoke to Maria in Spanish, her native tongue.

THE CASE OF THE BABY YAIR KIDNAPPING

Meanwhile, state and federal agents put out descriptions of the baby, the kidnapper, and the car for the media. It included a picture of baby Yair — a photo taken by his proud father shortly after the infant was born. Word of the abduction was spread through digital billboards, television, newspapers, and social networking sites on the Internet, such as Facebook, Twitter, and MySpace.

Family members, friends, and neighbors were questioned. "I never thought this could happen to us," said the baby's sleep-deprived dad, who was holding an energy drink to keep himself awake. "It's eating me inside, but I have to hold it together for my wife because she's in bad shape. I have to be strong for her."

Maria's cousin Jessenia Sigala told the agents she was certain the announcement sign in the front yard played a role in the abduction. "Nobody knew outside the family that Yair had been born," she said. "He just got out of the hospital last night. All I'm thinking about is the baby. The kidnapper didn't even take milk for him. Is he eating? Is he okay? Is he alive?"

Police canvassed the neighborhood of single-family brick homes searching for any witnesses. Neighbor Eric Peterson, who lived three doors down from Maria, told the investigators that on the afternoon of the kidnapping, Maria banged frantically on his door. "At first I thought she was playing a prank on me," he said. "But then I got a good look at her. She was covered from her head to her toe with blood with gashes on her neck and upper chest. She pleaded with me to rescue her children. She said there was a lady in the kitchen with a butcher knife, and that she had attacked her."

He said that by the time he ran over to Maria's house, the woman was speeding away in a dark blue car. Maria's daughter was standing outside the house, but the baby was gone. He brought the little girl with him back to his house and waited for the ambulance to take Maria to the hospital and for police to arrive.

After the FBI and state agencies set up tip lines, people began calling in from all over the country, thinking they had seen the suspect. Agents followed up on all the leads, hoping that one of them would eventually break open the case. One name showed promise — a woman who fit the description and, according to the tip, had left the area unexpectedly. Her name and photo were given out to the media as a "person of interest."

On Wednesday, the day after the crime, the FBI finally tracked her down at her grandparents' home near Buffalo, New York. Agents searched her car and the house, and questioned her. She denied any involvement and claimed the tipster was her ex-boyfriend who wanted to get even with her over a bad breakup. The investigation quickly cleared her.

Later that day, authorities held a press conference at the hospital where Maria was still being treated for her wounds and a collapsed lung. From her wheelchair and clutching a blanket on her lap, Maria begged the kidnapper to return baby Yair, and she asked the public for help in finding him. "I need my baby back," she said as tears from swollen eyes rolled down her cheeks. "He's five days old. He has a full head of black hair. He's kind of chubby. He has big cheeks. He has big eyes."

Back in her hospital room, Maria told Ahumada that she and her parents had left Mexico 14 years earlier and moved to Nashville in search of better job opportunities. Her parents eventually returned to Mexico, but by then, Maria had met her future husband and had started a new life and family in the town famously nicknamed Music City. Now, at what should have been one of the happiest times of her life, the new mom was suffering a parent's worst nightmare.

Maria soon began working with a police sketch artist to come up with a drawing of the suspect that authorities planned to give out to the media. Agents reached out to the Hispanic community with posters, pictures, and a message in Spanish about baby Yair's disappearance.

There had been no ransom notes or calls, and no demands from the abductor. Back at the command center, Agent Brown wondered, *What is the suspect's motive? Is she going to harm the baby or sell him or keep him?*

Kidnappings by strangers of infants up to six months old are relatively rare. Over the previous two years, there had been only 14 such cases nationwide, Cathy Nahirny, a senior analyst at the Center for Missing & Exploited Children, told agents in a conference call. She said it was doubtful any harm would come to the baby. Profiling the abductor, Nahirny told investigators, "She wants that baby. It's 'hers,' and she did it for the man in her life. She wants to keep that baby and the man." Nahirny added that kidnappers of infants tend to impersonate health-care or social-service workers or immigration agents to gain access to homes. They also case out health-care facilities to find new mothers to target.

Brown and Ahumada figured that the suspect must have had some sort of contact with Maria — with or without Maria's knowledge. Investigators established a timeline of Maria's activities on the day of the kidnapping to see if she might have come in contact with the suspect. They learned that Maria, who was accompanied by her cousin Jessenia, took the baby and her daughter to the Women, Infants and Children (WIC) health center and then to Walmart before returning home. Jessenia left them shortly before the abduction.

Brown thought the WIC, a federal program that provides basic necessities, such as formula, to poor women with children was the perfect place to find a child to abduct.

Authorities questioned staff members at the health center, asking if they had seen anything suspicious, but none had. The center had no surveillance cameras. But Walmart did, so the investigators were able to see video of Maria and her daughter, baby, and cousin in the store. There was no indication that anyone was following them.

However, when Brown and others examined the footage of surveillance cameras that scanned the parking lot, they found an intriguing clue. In the video, a dark blue Kia Spectra arrived seconds after Maria's car did and parked a short distance away. Later, when Maria and the others got back in her car and drove away, the Kia pulled out right behind her and followed her.

In a lucky break, the camera managed to get a grainy, partial image of the Kia's license plate, which was sent to a crime lab for enhancement. Because of the urgency of the case, the lab work that might have taken days to complete took only hours. The computer-enhanced photo showed the tag was Indiana license plate 138 GBG.

By Thursday morning — less than 48 hours after the kidnapping — agents learned the plate was from a Kia Spectra owned by the Hertz car rental company. Tracking it further, they found out that the Kia had been rented at the Nashville International Airport the night before the kidnapping.

Investigators went to the Hertz counter at the airport and examined surveillance video. It showed that the woman who rented the Kia fit the description of the kidnapper. Hertz provided credit-card and contact information of the renter: Tammy Renee Silas, of Ardmore, Alabama, a town about 85 miles south of Nashville.

According to Hertz, the car had been returned Tuesday evening — hours after the kidnapping — to Huntsville International Airport in Alabama, 25 miles from Ardmore.

THE CASE OF THE BABY YAIR KIDNAPPING

Because Hertz had Silas's cell phone number, agents were able to determine where and when she made her phone calls in the previous few days. One of her calls was relayed from a cell tower near Maria's home at about 11:15 A.M. on the day of the attack — just three hours before police received the 911 call.

Silas's credit- and debit-card transactions revealed that she had been at a gas station near the victim's house shortly before the abduction. Surveillance video from the station showed it was the same car that was spotted at Walmart. By tracking her transactions, the agents learned that Silas had been to a local bank to withdraw money from an outdoor ATM. When they watched surveillance video from the bank, they could clearly see an empty infant carrier next to her in the passenger seat.

By now, the agents were pretty confident that Silas was the person who had kidnapped Yair. Ahumada, who spoke to Maria every day, gave her encouraging news. "I have great confidence in all the agencies working together," Ahumada told Maria on Thursday, after the victim was released from the hospital. "It's looking promising that we'll find Yair for you."

Authorities put a surveillance team in place in Ardmore outside Silas's house on Friday. The big questions remained: Does Silas have the baby? Is he safe?

A background check revealed that Silas, 39, had a record of petty crimes, including drug possession. In 2002, she was arrested in two Ohio counties on charges of forgery and possessing criminal tools. She was sentenced to five years' probation for passing bad checks in Montgomery County, Ohio. In 2004, she was arrested in Nashville for violating probation from the forgery case and served a few months in jail. She also had gone by other names such as Tammy Hernandez, Tammy Gonzalez, Tammy Thomas, and Tammy Gwyn. Her aliases were linked to nearly 30 addresses in Alabama, Tennessee, Ohio, and a half dozen other states.

In 2004, while she was living in Nashville, Silas was questioned by police in the unsolved shooting death of her then boyfriend, Ramon Hernandez-Trejo. Authorities believed that he had been murdered by the Mexican Mafia or a drug dealer. The background check on Silas also revealed that at the time of the slaying, she lived within three miles of the house where Maria now lived.

Silas eventually moved to Ardmore, where she was now running a remodeling and roofing company with her current boyfriend, Martin Rodriguez.

At about 7 P.M., investigators observed Silas returning to her home in a pickup truck driven by Rodriguez. When she got out, she was carrying a bundle covered with a blanket. To the agents watching her, it looked like she was holding a baby, although they couldn't be sure.

Out of concern for the infant's safety, the agents didn't want to barge into the house in a show of force. Believing that Silas did not want to harm the baby, they thought they would take a low-key approach by conducting a "knock-and-talk."

Rodriguez answered the door and let them enter after they introduced themselves. They could see a pile of baby clothes on the dining-room table. When they asked to speak with Silas, he called out to her, and she walked into the front room holding an infant. In answer to their questions, Silas claimed that she had adopted the baby from a family member in Texas and named him Martin after Rodriguez. But agents could tell the infant looked exactly like the photo of Yair taken on the day he was born.

Because they had probable cause, they arrested Silas on the spot and took custody of the infant. Donning blue hospital gloves, an agent put the infant on a blanket, took off the baby's overalls, inspected him for any injuries (there were none), and looked for a specific birthmark (there was one). All the evidence said the baby was indeed the kidnapped Yair Carrillo.

They took a photo of "baby Martin" and sent it to Brown and other investigators who were with Maria at a relative's home. When shown the photo, Maria burst into tears and cried out, "That's my baby! That's my Yair!"

Told that Yair was safe and healthy, Maria, her husband, and children wept with happiness. She thanked and praised all the agents who helped save her newborn son and arrest the kidnapper.

Seeing how happy the family was, Brown thought, *It feels good to be part of an investigation that has been this success-ful.* Too many times it hadn't turned out that way.

Ahumada, who was at the command center monitoring the arrest through real-time communications, felt proud that she was part of a team that had rescued the infant and caught the culprit.

Back in Ardmore, agents questioned Rodriguez and Silas separately.

Rodriguez, who had been living with Silas for two years, told authorities Silas often discussed adopting a baby because she was unable to give birth. She told him she would soon be adopting the newborn of a pregnant cousin in Texas who was in jail on drug charges. Silas had spent weeks preparing for the baby's arrival, buying formula, clothes, blankets, and a bassinet.

A week before baby Yair's kidnapping, Rodriguez dropped Silas off at the Huntsville airport so she could catch a flight to Dallas, Texas. On Tuesday evening — hours after the abduction — she called him from the Huntsville airport, saying that she had adopted the baby in Texas and asked him to pick them up, which he did.

He told investigators he had no reason to doubt that the adoption of "Martin Jr." was anything but legitimate. "He was in good shape, and he didn't cry much," Rodriguez told them. "He ate lots of milk. Everything was fine. I didn't know anything was wrong until you showed up."

THE CASE OF THE BABY YAIR KIDNAPPING

Investigators found a baggage-claim sticker on Silas's luggage at her house, which showed that she had not flown from Dallas to Huntsville Tuesday evening. Instead, it revealed she had taken an American Airlines flight from Dallas to Nashville Monday evening, the day before the baby's kidnapping.

When Silas was questioned, she stuck with her adoption story until agents explained the evidence they had gathered against her. Then she came up with an outlandish accusation. She claimed she bought the infant for $25,000 from Maria and Jose Antonio. Even though it made little sense — why would Silas need to attack Maria if this were a baby-selling agreement? — authorities had to follow up on the outrageous claim.

Despite the accusation against Maria and Jose Antonio, Silas was formally charged on Saturday with kidnapping and told she faced a sentence of life in prison.

That same day, baby Yair was given a thorough examination by a physician who determined the infant was well cared for. After a DNA test confirmed his identity, Yair was driven back to Nashville for a reunion with his family at the offices of the Tennessee Department of Children's Services (DCS). To the heartache of the family, however, the meeting was much too brief. Once again, Yair was taken away, this time by DCS officials. Not only that, but they took Maria's other three children, too, and put them all in foster care while Silas's accusation was checked out.

THE CASE OF THE BABY YAIR KIDNAPPING

Not finding a shred of evidence to support the suspect's claim, the investigation confirmed she had lied about buying the baby. The children were then reunited with Maria and her husband Tuesday afternoon — exactly one week after Yair had been kidnapped.

Meanwhile, several of Silas's neighbors and acquaintances, who were questioned by authorities, couldn't believe she was an abductor. One person said Silas was someone you could always count on. A neighbor described Silas as "the nicest person," adding that "she said she couldn't have children, but didn't say anything about wanting a child so badly" that she would kidnap one.

A few weeks after Yair had been rescued, Ahumada talked to Maria.

"I never lost hope that I was going to get my baby back," Maria told her. "I can't thank the FBI enough for helping find Yair."

The agent replied, "It was a great effort by everyone involved. I am proud to have been a part of the investigation and even more pleased that this was a case that had a very happy ending."

On February 14, 2011, Silas peaded guilty to kidnapping Yair. Five months later, she was sentenced to 20 years in prison with an additional five years of supervised probation. She also was ordered to pay more than $36,000 to the family.

THE CASE OF THE BABY YAIR KIDNAPPING

On the day of Silas's sentencing, Maria told the court that Yair was a happy 22-month-old who didn't appear to suffer any emotional scars from the trauma. However, the rest of her family was affected by the kidnapping. She said her three older children continued to struggle in school and suffer nightmares. The family never went back to live in the house where Yair was taken. In fact, Maria said she could hardly stand to drive down the street because of all the bad memories. She still bore the scars of the attack, including a thin vertical line running down the ridge of her nose. "It's impossible to put down on paper the suffering," she said in a statement in federal court. "But nothing compares to the happiness of having our son once again in our arms."

After receiving permission to address Silas, Maria told the defendant, "For all the harm you have done to me, for trying to take my life away . . . I forgive you."

THE CASE OF THE STOLEN MOON ROCKS

*G*reetings. My name is Orb Robinson from Tampa, Florida. I have in my possession a rare multi-karat moon rock I am trying to find a buyer for. The laws surrounding this type of exchange are known, so I will be straightforward about wanting to find a private buyer. If you, or someone you know, would be interested in such an exchange, please let me know. Thank you.

Orb Robinson

The email, dated May 7, 2002, intrigued Axel Emmermann, an amateur mineralogist from Antwerp, Belgium. He had never heard of this Orb Robinson, who had sent the same email to several members of the Mineralogy Club of Antwerp, whose addresses were on the group's website. Emmermann grew suspicious. He knew it was illegal in the United States for anyone other than the federal government to sell or possess rocks from the moon because they are so scientifically valuable.

Convinced that the email sender was either a con man trying to sell fake moon rocks or a thief who actually stole them, Emmermann decided to play along. He wrote back that he might be interested if they were affordable and if Orb could prove they really came from the moon.

Before hearing back from Orb, Emmermann alerted the FBI's antifraud team in Tampa of a possible scam. Special Agent Lawrence Wolfenden then launched an investigation in which Emmermann agreed to assist Special Agent Nick Nance in setting up a sting operation.

At first, Nance suspected this was a case of Internet fraud. Most of the 842 pounds of lunar rocks that had been collected from all the successful Apollo moon missions from 1969 through 1972 were safely stored at NASA's Johnson Space Center (JSC) in Houston, Texas. The federal government gave the remaining samples to officials and scientists of other countries.

With help from the FBI about what to say, Emmermann exchanged several emails with Orb concerning the price of the moon rocks as well as how the transaction would be handled. As part of the sting, Emmermann said that he would wire $100,000 to his brother, Kurt, and sister-in-law,

Lynn Briley, in Pennsylvania. They would pay Orb for the moon rocks in cash at a time and place in the United States to be decided later. All future negotiations would be handled via email through Lynn, whose hobby was mineralogy. Orb agreed to Emmermann's wishes — not knowing that the Lynn he would be emailing was really Nance.

The agent chose to pose online as a woman because of the expertise of Special Agent Lynn Billings of the FBI's Sarasota office. She had a degree in geology, so Nance figured she could help him sound credible with Orb. Nance and Billings had worked together on previous cases, although none as unique as this one. Billings would pose as Lynn Briley in any face-to-face meetings with Orb. The FBI even created a background for the fake Lynn: She was an American who worked as a publisher in Philadelphia and was an amateur rock collector. Her Belgian-born husband, Kurt, would be portrayed by Wolfenden. To make the couple seem more believable to Orb, the two agents had their picture taken at a restaurant in case they needed to show him a photo of themselves together.

Nance, who had experience portraying fictitious people on the Internet in investigations, began an email dialogue with the suspect: "Yes, Orb! I will handle this for Axel. He has explained to me a good bit about what we are doing — and the need for caution and discretion! Lynn."

While Nance, posing as Lynn, was communicating with

Orb through emails, the FBI checked the IP (Internet provider) addresses of the suspect and traced them to public computers at the University of Utah library. Other emails from Orb were eventually traced to public computers at a bank and a library in Houston. But the case took a more ominous turn when the FBI discovered that emails from Orb were now coming from an IP address at the Johnson Space Center, where most moon rocks were kept.

This no longer appeared to be the scheme of a small-time con artist, but rather that of a crafty criminal inside the space center itself. *Orb — probably not his real name — might actually have access to the moon rocks*, Nance thought. *This could be the real deal. He might be trying to find buyers before stealing the samples.*

The FBI could not nail down which one of the space center's hundreds of computers Orb was using.

Not knowing who at the JSC might be involved, Nance was reluctant to talk to officials there because he didn't want to arouse suspicion. Instead, he contacted Patty Koenig (now Searle) near the Kennedy Space Center in Melbourne, Florida. Koenig was a special agent for the inspector general's office that investigates crimes for NASA. She agreed to work on the case with Nance because she had better contacts and easier access to information at the JSC than he did.

Nance examined the academic calendar year for the University of Utah, in Salt Lake City, and saw that finals had just finished. *Maybe this Orb is a professor or grad student who has some kind of grant or internship with NASA at the space center,* Nance thought. The agent asked Koenig to find out who at the JSC had a connection with Utah.

She learned that a Utah professor was beginning his third summer working on a project at the space center and had taken a graduate assistant with him this time. *The professor has been there before and has a lay of the land*, Nance thought. *He might be our prime suspect.*

After several emails between Orb and "Lynn," they agreed to meet at an undetermined restaurant in Orlando, Florida, on Saturday, July 20 — ironically, the thirty-third anniversary of man's first walk on the moon by Neil Armstrong.

Nance needed Orb to bring all the moon rocks he had — assuming he actually had them. If Orb held any back, the FBI might never find them. So, as Lynn, the agent emailed Orb: "If these prove to be authentic, I'm sure more of my mineralogical society friends would be interested, and we can pool the money and buy the rest of them from you. Would you please bring all the samples so I can take pictures of them and send them back to Axel so he would have something to show his friends?"

Orb agreed to the request, saying in an email, "As we approach the meeting date, I will provide you with proof, authenticating that these samples are real."

THE CASE OF THE STOLEN MOON ROCKS

The week before the meeting, Lynn emailed, "Orb, very excited about next weekend. Speaking of the restaurant, how will I recognize you?"

Orb responded, "I will be wearing a black shirt with a dolphin-pendant necklace at the meeting at 6 P.M., so you should recognize me."

The magnitude of the case took on added importance on the Monday before the meeting. Nance received a phone call from Koenig, who told him, "You aren't going to believe this, but thieves broke into a scientist's lab at the Johnson Space Center over the weekend and stole a safe containing Apollo lunar samples. I told my contact there, 'I think I know who stole your safe — Orb Robinson.'"

The next day, Orb emailed Lynn that he had proof that the rocks he wanted to sell her were authentic. Lynn gave him a fax number she said was of the company she worked for. But it was really an undercover fax line to an FBI office in Pennsylvania.

On Wednesday, Orb faxed various documents that catalogued and listed the characteristics of each of the 101 grams (about 3.5 ounces) of moon rocks that had been in the stolen safe of noted NASA scientist Dr. Everett Gibson. Nance forwarded the fax to Koenig, who confirmed the documents were real. The FBI was now confident that the person who had been emailing Lynn was the same person involved in the theft of the most valuable rocks in the world.

As Lynn, Nance emailed, "Orb, all we can say is WOW!!!"

THE CASE OF THE STOLEN MOON ROCKS

With a suspect and clear evidence of a crime, the FBI prepared an arrest warrant for the culprit. The problem was, the Bureau didn't know the person's true identity, so the warrant was issued for "John Doe, also known as Orb Robinson."

Now it was time to set the trap. Nance and Koenig went to Orlando to find a safe public place to conduct the transaction. They chose Italianni's restaurant on busy International Drive. In an email confirming the time and place, Orb said he first wanted to meet Lynn alone before having his friends and her husband join them at the restaurant.

Meanwhile, Special Agent Lynn Billings, who would play the undercover role of Lynn Briley at the meeting, examined all the emails that Nance and Orb had exchanged in case Orb referred to any of them. She also studied the physical composition and characteristics of lunar rocks so she could talk with Orb in depth about them.

Billings, who had done limited undercover work before, felt up to the challenge. After getting her geology degree at the University of Kansas and working in that field for a couple of years, she went back to college and earned a mechanical engineering degree. She then worked for the Department of Energy at a nuclear weapons complex until, at the urging of friends at the FBI, she joined the Bureau in 1996.

Hours before the meeting, Nance led an arrest briefing with the nearly two dozen agents who were now part of the sting operation. He passed out photos of the suspects —

the University of Utah professor, who was in his forties, and his grad student. "We don't know for certain if they are the thieves," he told his colleagues. "But they likely will be the ones who will show up."

Heading to the restaurant, the agents were caught in a thunderstorm that caused a massive traffic jam. As a result, they arrived at the restaurant 15 minutes late, and there was no sign of Orb. Nance hoped the suspect was delayed by the traffic and not by chickening out.

Koenig, two male agents, and a female agent from Nance's squad posed as couples in the restaurant. Their job was to observe the meeting and protect their colleague and everyone else in the place in case of trouble. Billings went to the bar area to wait for Orb.

Outside the restaurant, Nance and other agents, including a surveillance squad, got in position. Special Agent Lawrence Wolfenden, who would play Emmermann's brother, Kurt, was in a car, waiting to get the word from Billings to join her.

Billings kept her eyes peeled on the door, hoping the professor would show up at any moment. After about ten minutes, a handsome man in his twenties walked in. He was wearing a black shirt with a dolphin pendant, and looked nothing like the older man in the FBI photo she had been expecting. The young man introduced himself as Orb Robinson.

Billings was secretly wearing a wire to record the conversation and also a radio transmitter so that Nance and the others outside could hear everything. She told Orb, "It's nice to finally put a face to someone who I have been emailing with."

The two went to a table, ordered dinner, and exchanged pleasantries, but neither wanted to divulge too much at first. The agent told him, "I'm sure Orb isn't your real name." He nodded but declined to give it. Billings didn't press the issue because she didn't want him to get suspicious. *We'll get his name anyway when we arrest him*, she thought.

She asked him how he had obtained the moon rocks. To her surprise, Orb talked for a full ten minutes about his daring crime — NASA's biggest case of grand theft involving space material.

He said he was a college intern at the Johnson Space Center and came up with the scheme after visiting Dr. Gibson's laboratory. The unsuspecting scientist had agreed to show Orb the moon rocks, which were kept in a special 600-pound safe that looked like a file cabinet. Orb noticed that Dr. Gibson first pulled out a card from the slot on the front of a specific drawer and flipped the card over. Reading numbers printed on the back, the scientist turned the dial on the combination lock several times and opened the drawer. After putting the card back, he took out a tray of small glass tubes containing tiny samples of moon rocks.

Orb told Lynn that once he decided to steal the lunar samples, he had a friend, Gordon, find a buyer overseas, who turned out to be Axel Emmermann. Orb then recruited his girlfriend, Tiffany, and another girl, Shae — who, like him, were both intelligent college interns at the JSC — to help him pull off the heist. They borrowed an SUV and late Saturday night drove to the space center, where they showed their credentials to guards, giving them access to the center.

The more Orb talked about the crime to Lynn, the more animated he got. He told her that while Shae acted as a look-out, he and Tiffany walked to the building where Dr. Gibson's laboratory was located. Having worked in the building, Orb knew the code that gained them entry. However, the door to Dr. Gibson's lab was another matter. Opening it also required a special code — pressing four buttons on a wall pad in a certain sequence — which he didn't know. But after 30 minutes of trial and error, Orb figured it out. Once inside the lab, he lifted the card from the front of the cabinet drawer and, using the numbers on the back, tried to open the safe. But it remained locked. He came to realize that the numbers weren't the actual combination; they were a prompt that helped Dr. Gibson remember the combination. So Orb went to plan B, which meant they had to steal the safe. Fortunately for him, he had the foresight to bring along a dolly. After a struggle with the heavy safe, he and Tiffany wheeled it to their vehicle without being seen. Then the three burglars drove to a motel in the nearby town of Webster, Texas, where they had bought some power tools. They used an electric skill saw to cut off the metal locking pins of the safe's draw-ers and pulled out the treasure trove of moon rocks. Also inside were the documents that Orb later faxed to prove the lunar samples were real.

The more he talks, the more pleased he seems with himself, Billings thought. *I need to keep him talking, which shouldn't be too hard because he has a big ego.*

"We were worried about all the noise we were making in the motel room while we were trying to break open the safe, but no one complained," he told Billings.

"Well, this is very nice," she told him.

Orb took a deep breath, stared at her, and said, "I just hope you're not wearing a wire."

The agent laughed off such a notion, trying to ease any suspicion he might have.

"You know what my girlfriend said today?" Orb said. "She's like . . . they could make a movie of my life."

"You sound very adventurous," Billings replied. "And your girlfriend sounds adventurous, too."

During a natural lull in the conversation, the agent mentally went down a checklist of things she wanted Orb to say on the recording. Needing him to admit that he was the one sending the emails, she steered the talk in that direction until he acknowledged that he was the sender.

Even though the recording device was still working, the separate radio transmitter she was wearing had malfunctioned, so Nance and his colleagues couldn't eavesdrop on the conversation. However, one of the agents sitting at a table nearby phoned Nance that Billings was talking to someone who didn't fit the description of the professor but was wearing a black shirt with a dolphin pendant.

The FBI's plan called for "Kurt" and "Lynn" to take Orb to their motel room next door to the restaurant, where a takedown team was waiting to make the arrest. But Orb nixed the idea of closing the deal in the couple's room. He explained that the moon rocks were in his room at the Sheraton Hotel, about a mile away, and insisted on completing the transaction there.

Orb then said he wanted Lynn to meet two of his accomplices, who had dropped him off at the restaurant and were now at another table. She agreed on the condition that her husband, Kurt, who supposedly was at the motel, would join them as well. Then she excused herself and called Wolfenden. Billings told him that after everyone met one another, they all would go to Orb's room at the Sheraton.

Wolfenden relayed the information to Nance and then walked into the restaurant. Pretending to be Belgian, Wolfenden talked with a fake Dutch accent. Because the agent didn't speak Dutch (one of Belgium's three official languages), he was prepared in case Orb tested him. If Orb talked to him in Dutch, Wolfenden would reply with a couple Dutch sentences he had memorized: "Very good. You speak a little Dutch, but my wife does not, and prefers I not hold private conversations in front of her." Fortunately, Wolfenden didn't need to speak any Dutch.

THE CASE OF THE STOLEN MOON ROCKS

Wolfenden had $100,000 in cash in a briefcase and offered to show it to Orb, but Orb didn't want him to open it in such a public setting, saying, "I'll take your word for it."

When the two undercover agents were introduced to Orb's girlfriend, Tiffany, and his friend Gordon, most members of the FBI team outside the restaurant rushed to the Sheraton, where they planned to arrest the culprits. Surveillance units remained behind.

Because Orb didn't give a room number, the FBI didn't know exactly where the deal would take place. Nance was concerned there might be armed people in the room, putting Billings and Wolfenden in danger. There was also the possibility that once Orb and the two undercover agents got into the elevator, Nance and his fellow agents would be running up and down the hallways trying to find them. So a senior FBI official ordered the takedown teams, "Don't let them get into the hotel. Arrest them in the parking lot as soon as they get out of the car."

Back at the restaurant, Orb admitted he was too excited to finish his meal and offered it to Tiffany, who acted giddy as she polished off the plate.

"This is a life-changing event," Wolfenden told them. They agreed — not knowing just how life-changing it would be for them.

After a short chat, Gordon and Tiffany went in one car while Orb rode with Billings and Wolfenden toward the

Sheraton. On the drive over there, Billings was worried that the recording of her conversation with Orb had been drowned out by the noise from patrons' conversations and the restaurant's loud background music. Still wearing the wire, she appealed to his vanity to get him to repeat details of the heist to Wolfenden in the car, which was a much quieter environment. Orb was so proud of his crime that he didn't hesitate to tell Wolfenden all about it while Billings recorded his incriminating words.

As the car pulled into the hotel parking lot, Orb could barely contain his anticipation of selling the moon rocks. But his enthusiasm turned to anguish the moment he stepped out of the car, because that's when the takedown team arrested him. He was so stunned he didn't say anything at first. The FBI quickly determined the mastermind's real name — Thad Roberts, 25.

When his friends parked in another part of the lot, Nance, Koenig, and an agent blocked the car and pounced on them. "FBI!" barked Nance. "Hands up! You're under arrest!"

"Whoa, d-did we commit a traffic violation?" Gordon stammered. "Whatever we did, we didn't mean to do it."

"Turn around," Nance ordered. Then he and the other agents put them in handcuffs and separated them. The two were identified as Tiffany Fowler, 22, an intern in NASA's tissue-culture laboratory, and Gordon McWhorter, 25, of Salt Lake City, a student at the University of Utah.

THE CASE OF THE STOLEN MOON ROCKS

The fourth person involved in the theft, Shae Saur, 19, a member of a student team that created a zero-gravity pollination experiment for NASA, was later arrested in Houston.

After obtaining a search warrant, Nance, Billings, and Wolfenden entered the hotel room, where they found a tackle box on the floor next to the bed, partially draped by the bedspread. Nance put on gloves and gently opened the box. Inside were the priceless lunar samples. Each rock was labeled and in a glass container that looked like a pill bottle cushioned by cotton balls to prevent breakage. Also in the tackle box was a specimen from an asteroid (a space rock that once orbited the sun between Mars and Jupiter).

Billings was awed when she saw the moon rocks. At first she wondered whether they were counterfeit, but the documents accompanying the samples confirmed they were real. "These are extraordinary," she marveled.

In addition, the agents found a disposable camera that contained photos taken by Fowler the night the safe was stolen. The pictures showed the burglars using power tools to break the safe open. She had shot the photos so Orb could prove to Lynn that the moon rocks came from the safe at the Johnson Space Center.

Nance was pleased that the sting operation had worked to perfection. *Although we were wrong about who we thought was behind the theft, at least we got the samples back and arrested the people responsible for the crime*, he told himself.

McWhorter, Fowler, and Saur posted bond and were released from jail. But no one put up bail money for Roberts. While behind bars, he offered to cooperate with the FBI, hoping that would lead to a lighter sentence. Nance and Koenig interviewed him three times, and though he didn't act contrite, he did not volunteer much information at first.

"Tell me what you know and I'll tell you whether you're right or wrong," he told them on their initial visit.

"I'm not playing games," Nance responded. "Either you help us or you don't."

Eventually, Roberts became more cooperative and explained how he ended up a thief: At the University of Utah, Roberts studied geology, physics, and geophysics, and led a weekly star-gazing group at the school's observatory. In 2001, the overachiever was accepted into NASA's elite summer Cooperative Education Program for the brightest college science students. He was assigned to the JSC, where he hoped eventually to get picked for astronaut training. In his second summer there, he worked as a support diver in the Neutral Buoyancy Laboratory, helping astronauts in space suits practice zero-gravity tasks in a 40-foot-deep pool.

When he hatched his plan to steal the moon rocks, he gave McWhorter the job of finding a buyer through the

Internet, using the fake name of Orb Robinson. Knowing that the possession or sale of moon rocks was illegal in the United States, McWhorter contacted amateur mineralogists in Belgium. And that's when Axel Emmermann responded to the offer and tipped off the FBI.

Roberts soon took over the role of Orb Robinson in emails with Nance posing as Lynn Briley. Once a deal was reached to sell the moon rocks, Roberts and the women stole the safe that contained the lunar samples — which were later valued at more than $20 million — from Dr. Gibson's laboratory. When the thieves opened the safe, they took the rocks and the documentation and threw the rest of the contents into a Dumpster. They put the samples in a fishing tackle box and hid it in Saur's storage shed. The next day, they went back to their daily routine at the space center.

While Saur stayed behind in Texas, Roberts and Fowler took the tackle box and drove through the night from Houston to Orlando, where they met up with McWhorter. Later that day in the restaurant, they expected to hit the jackpot but ended up in jail instead, thanks to the FBI's clever sting operation.

In praising the work of his fellow agents, Wolfenden told the media how vital it was that the lunar samples were recovered: "The United States spent millions of dollars getting these rocks. This isn't just a treasure for our country, but for all of humanity. It's our universe, our history."

*   *   *

THE CASE OF THE STOLEN MOON ROCKS

In 2003, Fowler and Saur pleaded guilty to charges of conspiracy to commit theft and interstate transportation of stolen property. They were sentenced to six months of house arrest and three years of probation.

McWhorter, who declined to plead guilty, went to trial, where he was convicted of conspiracy and served four and a half years in federal prison.

When FBI agents searched Roberts's Salt Lake City apartment, they found fossils he had stolen from the Utah Museum of Natural History, resulting in an additional charge. He pleaded guilty to all charges and served more than eight years in federal prison. While locked up, he wrote a 700-page book on quantum space theory.

When Nance and Koenig interviewed Fowler, she said Roberts liked to think of himself as a James Bond on a secret mission, and he viewed the heist as an adventure.

"Thad was a very bright, motivated student," Nance says. "He had his foot in the door with NASA and was well on his way to reaching his goal of becoming an astronaut. And then in this one greedy event, in one fell swoop, he threw his life away."

Dr. Gibson said six irreplaceable notebooks of handwritten notes documenting 33 years of research were in the stolen safe. Roberts repeatedly denied seeing them, even though photos taken the night of the theft show some of the notebooks on the floor of the motel room after the safe was opened. They were never recovered.

THE CASE OF THE STOLEN MOON ROCKS

In gratitude of Emmermann's honesty, integrity, and cooperation with the FBI, an asteroid was named after him.

A week after the theft, Wolfenden sent an email to Emmermann, which said in part:

I'm writing to let you know that your assistance has been instrumental, in fact, essential, in recovering the lunar samples. . . . If you hadn't contacted us, I'm certain that Orb would have kept looking for a buyer for the moon rocks. Unfortunately, not everyone has your integrity. Someone would have taken him up on his offer, and what can certainly be considered a "National Treasure" would have been lost to the U.S. Government, possibly forever. . . .

Your brother,

"Kurt"

THE CASE OF THE
JOE COOL MURDERS

Special Agent David Nunez faced a seemingly impossible task: He and his team of investigators had to uncover enough evidence for federal prosecutors to convict two cold-blooded killers — even though there were no bodies, no weapons, and no witnesses.

The five-year FBI veteran was assigned to the Miami Maritime Squad, which is responsible for investigating crimes on the high seas involving American citizens. Early Monday morning, September 24, 2007, he received a call from the Coast Guard with disturbing news: On the previous Saturday afternoon, a 47-foot charter sport fishing boat, the *Joe Cool*, left Miami with a crew of four and two passengers bound for the Bahamian island of Bimini, 53 miles away. The vessel never reached its destination. Sunday afternoon, family members alerted the Coast Guard, which launched a search. A few hours later, a cutter found the boat — abandoned, blood-splattered, and in a mess — drifting aimlessly about 30 miles north of Cuba, far from its intended course. It was obvious that a violent struggle had occurred on board.

Now it was Monday morning, and the Coast Guard had just rescued two men in a life raft a half mile from where the charter boat was discovered. The pair told rescuers that Cuban pirates had hijacked the *Joe Cool* and killed the crew but spared the two men, allowing them to leave in a raft.

Nunez knew there was no time to lose. *I need to get there fast before saltwater destroys any evidence,* he thought. As the lead case agent, he quickly assembled a unit that included two members of the Evidence Response Team as well as Coast Guard Investigative Service Special Agent Rick Blais. They sped to Opa-locka Executive Airport and took a Coast Guard jet to Marathon in the Florida Keys. Then they hopped aboard a bright orange Dolphin helicopter that flew to the Coast Guard cutter *Confidence* in the Florida Straits.

Moments after landing on the back of the ship, the investigators were briefed by the command staff on the latest developments: The two survivors were Kirby Archer, 35, of Strawberry, Arkansas, and Guillermo Zarabozo, 19, of Hialeah, Florida. Archer was found carrying $2,200 in $100 bills. There was also an outstanding fugitive warrant for his arrest for the theft of more than $90,000 in cash and checks in January from a Walmart in Batesville, Arkansas, where he was an assistant manager before vanishing.

Zarabozo's Florida driver's license was found on the *Joe Cool* along with a laptop, computer accessories, luggage, a daily planner, clothing, cameras, a cell phone, and equipment worth tens of thousands of dollars. A handcuff key was also spotted on the vessel's bow. Empty bottles of cleaning fluids were scattered on the deck, as if someone had tried to wipe up the crime scene.

The crew aboard the helicopter that rescued the two men reported that the life raft had six pieces of black luggage, one of which contained knives, a blowgun, and darts. The raft was retrieved and brought aboard the *Confidence*. The most troubling report was that the survivors claimed the charter boat captain, his wife, and the two other crew members had been shot and dumped at sea by the Cuban pirates.

The victims were Captain Jake Branam, 27; his wife, Kelley, 30; boat mechanic and Jake's half brother, Scott Gamble, 35; and first mate Sammy Kairy, 27.

Unfortunately for the investigators, by the time they reached the *Confidence*, a storm had blown in, whipping up waves and dumping sheets of rain. It was a nightmare for the team to find clues because the rain and saltwater threatened to ruin evidence, including possible DNA. The heavy seas also made it too dangerous for the Evidence Response

Team to work, so a crew from another cutter secured lines to the *Joe Cool* and began towing it to Miami.

On board the *Confidence*, Nunez and Blais began questioning the men separately. The investigators sat down with Zarabozo first to hear his version of events. The strapping young man seemed calm, although he had the nervous habit of rubbing his dark-haired crew cut before answering questions. Nunez noticed that Zarabozo couldn't seem to look either agent in the eye.

Zarabozo told them he was a private security guard who had met Archer on a job, but couldn't provide any details of where or when. He said the two men had booked a boat trip to Bimini to meet their girlfriends. When Nunez pressed him for details, Zarabozo couldn't come up with their cell phone numbers, physical descriptions, how and where they were to meet, or even the name of one of them.

"Tell me about the hijacking," Nunez said.

"I was on the fly bridge [the highest deck] with the captain and his wife when I overheard a radio call from a vessel in distress," Zarabozo replied. "The captain went to rescue the fishing boat. When we pulled up next to it, we saw three Cuban men, and two of them jumped onto the charter boat. One climbed up to the fly bridge and shot the captain and he fell to the deck below. His wife started freaking out and acting hysterically, so he shot her twice in the side and she fell next to her husband."

Zarabozo said that when the two remaining crew members refused the pirates' orders to toss the captain and his wife overboard, they were shot, too. Zarabozo claimed that he and Archer begged for their lives and then, at gunpoint, the pirates made the two throw all four bodies into the sea.

"The captain was still alive when I threw him overboard," Zarabozo told Nunez, adding that the pirates forced him to clean up all the blood after the shootings.

The agent found it odd that Zarabozo related the horrific events in such a matter-of-fact way with little emotion. He then asked, "Why did the pirates kill the crew?"

"Because they were witnesses."

"Yes, but you and Archer were witnesses, too."

"I'm Cuban, and they were Cuban, so they let me live."

"Well, what about the white guy [Archer] you were with?"

"Oh, they needed him to drive the boat."

"Okay, so these guys board the vessel with the intent of stealing it and yet they didn't bring anyone who could drive the boat? And then they kill the one person who could operate the boat?" *This sounds ridiculous*, Nunez thought. *He's lying. Too many pieces of his story aren't making any sense.*

Zarabozo said that Archer was then forced to drive the boat toward Cuba, but when it ran out of fuel, the pirates called another vessel, which picked them up and left him and Archer to fend for themselves. "The pirates jumped onto another boat and told us, 'You're on your own,' and then they left," Zarabozo told Nunez. "We decided we had a better chance of being rescued if we got in the life raft."

By now, Zarabozo was becoming more uneasy, and Nunez was becoming more doubtful. *He's got that deer-in-the-headlights look*, the agent thought. *He can't even make anything up.*

When asked to describe the pirates, Zarabozo said they were dark-haired men who wore polo shirts and jeans.

After questioning Zarabozo for a couple of hours, Nunez and Blais interviewed Archer, who had frosted dark blond hair and a goatee. Although he told a story similar to Zarabozo's, certain key details were different, especially the order of events during the murders. The two suspects also gave conflicting descriptions of the pirates. Archer claimed that two of them wore T-shirts and shorts while the older one had on a T-shirt and long, dark cargo pants. He described the murders in such a way that left the FBI agent convinced the suspect was a psychopath. In Archer's version, it was the captain's wife who was still alive when flung overboard. Archer laughed as he told how she was then eaten by sharks.

Annoyed and disgusted with his demeanor, Nunez snapped, "And you think this is funny?"

Archer shrugged and continued to laugh.

Neither suspect could explain to Nunez and Blais how they were able to keep money, clothes, and other things after the pirates had hijacked the boat. By their very nature, pirates rob people, and yet, in this case, they didn't take the boat, the money, or any of the expensive fishing and electronic gear.

When the agents were through with the initial round of questioning, Nunez told Blais, "There are so many inconsistencies, it's clear they are lying."

Meanwhile, the Coast Guard reported it hadn't received or intercepted any distress calls like the suspects claimed the pirates used to lure the *Joe Cool*. No ships in the area heard any such mayday calls, either.

On the way back to Miami on the *Confidence,* Nunez and Blais knew they could hold Archer in custody because of the Arkansas arrest warrant. But the agents didn't have any legal reason for keeping Zarabozo, who had no criminal record. "We don't have enough to lock him up," Nunez told Blais. "If we turn him loose, he'll be a flight risk."

Later, Blais was on the deck of the cutter, making small talk with Zarabozo. Pointing to the towed *Joe Cool*, Blais asked, "Did you like being on the *Joe Cool*? Is it a nice fishing boat?"

Zarabozo folded his arms and replied, "I've never seen that boat in my life."

It was an obvious lie. Not only was his driver's license on board the charter boat, but security cameras at the Miami Beach Marina showed the two suspects boarding the vessel the previous Saturday. The FBI then charged him with lying to a federal agent. At least now authorities could hold the pair while the agents built a case against them.

Despite an intensive air-sea search that covered 1,900 square miles, the Coast Guard could find no trace of the victims.

Without the bodies, witnesses, or weapons, Nunez knew that proving Archer and Zarabozo were high-seas murderers was going to be extremely difficult. The Bureau told Nunez to work only on this one case full time. (It would end up consuming the next 18 months of his life.) To assist in the investigation, he assembled a team that included a dozen agents and police officers from various departments.

Nunez and his team began conducting interviews with more than 100 of the suspects' friends, relatives, neighbors, ex-coworkers, and acquaintances. Investigators checked the suspects' credit-card purchases and cell phone calls to track their movements and find out when, where, and with whom they were talking. Their homes were searched.

Nunez learned that Archer was a U.S. Army police investigator in the 1990s in Guantanamo Bay, Cuba, but he got in trouble for going AWOL (absent without leave). After he left the army with a less-than-honorable discharge, he moved to Arkansas, where he lived with his second wife and two young sons. But the marriage ended in divorce.

In January 2007, the Arkansas State Police ordered him to take a polygraph exam for a domestic-abuse investigation. The evening before the scheduled test, Archer, who was the night-shift customer-service manager of Walmart in Batesville, collected all the money from the cash registers, went to a back room, and stuffed it in an empty microwave box. He took the box to the checkout counter and acted like he was paying for a microwave with his employee discount. Then he walked out, tricking employees into thinking he had bought the appliance when in fact the box contained $92,600 in stolen money. He borrowed his uncle's van and disappeared after first texting his third wife, "I really messed up this time."

Arkansas authorities didn't know at the time that for the next seven months, Archer was living in Hialeah, Florida. He had moved in with a family he had befriended in Cuba before they had immigrated to the United States. He played the part of a mysterious government agent by wearing nice clothes and mirrored sunglasses, always carrying a briefcase, driving a fast car, and dropping hints of secret missions.

Zarabozo, who was born in Cuba, came to Hialeah with his parents when he was nine years old. He became a Boy Scout, and at Hialeah High School, he joined the ROTC, a military-based program for students. Friends and teachers said he was a good student and a polite young man who wouldn't harm anyone. After graduation, he started freelancing for several security firms as a private guard. Licensed to carry a gun, Zarabozo was fascinated with weapons and often spent time at a

Hialeah firing range. Relatives said he hoped to become a police officer. In fact, a search of his house uncovered an orientation letter from the Miami Police Training Center for recruits.

Meanwhile, investigators found important evidence on the *Joe Cool*. Blood smears were on the deck, the walls, a power cord, and other items. Lab technicians were able to determine that DNA in the blood matched those of the four victims.

Also recovered on the boat were four empty shell casings. The Miami-Dade Police Department's laboratory determined the casings came from a 9-mm GLOCK handgun. The investigation discovered that as a licensed armed security guard, Zarabozo was issued a GLOCK by Pinkerton Security. Normally at the end of a specific job, security guards must hand in their weapon. But no records could be found that showed Zarabozo ever returned his weapon to Pinkerton.

In a search of his home, federal agents discovered a box of ammunition Zarabozo had bought in February 2007. The bullets were the same kind that came from the four spent shell casings.

The search also uncovered a receipt from Lou's Police Supply for a magazine that fit a 9-mm GLOCK. It was dated September 12, 2007 — just ten days before the murders. When agents went to the store where the magazine was purchased, they saw surveillance video that showed the two suspects buying the magazine along with another for a SIG

SAUER 9-mm handgun. "We're never going to find the murder weapon because it's at the bottom of the ocean," Nunez told his team. "But we are giving the prosecution some very strong circumstantial evidence."

The agents also found an empty handcuff box at the home of Zarabozo's mother. Investigators believed the small key found aboard the *Joe Cool* fit a pair of handcuffs that once was in the box.

Having secured subpoenas, investigators examined Zarabozo's computer hard drive and uncovered incriminating messages and emails. They found he had done Internet searches on such topics as Havana, Cuba, and marinas in the weeks leading up to the murders. He had even mapped routes from Florida to Cuba.

When investigators went through his MySpace account, they discovered he had several revealing communications with his girlfriend. He told her he was working on a secret government job that would keep him in Cuba for a year or more. It would make him a lot of money so that when he returned to Florida, he would be able to take care of her in style.

Archer's final MySpace entry was on the morning that he and Zarabozo boarded the *Joe Cool*. In a lengthy goodbye to the family he was staying with, Archer said he was leaving for a secret job. He wrote, "I'm good at what I do and I'll be fine . . . I know I've been secretive, that's the way I am, and there's no changing that, especially now."

Nunez learned from Jonathan Branam, co-owner of the *Joe Cool*, that the suspects approached the boat's first mate on Friday, September 21. They posed as surveyors who had finished their assignment early and wanted to join their girlfriends, who were already in Bimini. Archer claimed that his girlfriend had accidentally packed his passport in her suitcase, so he couldn't fly there. Instead, he wanted to charter the boat for a one-way trip to Bimini, where his girlfriend would meet the *Joe Cool* at the dock and give him his passport. Jake agreed to take them because it was quick, easy money. He convinced his wife, Kelley, to leave their four-month-old son and two-and-a-half-year-old daughter with their grandparents and come along for the ride.

Surveillance video at the marina showed the two suspects boarding the boat on that fateful Saturday afternoon. They arrived 15 minutes late, toting six black duffel bags. Jonathan, who stopped by to collect the money, later told investigators that Archer "seemed like a real nice guy, very likable . . . I didn't really see anything wrong."

At 3:49 P.M., the *Joe Cool* shoved off from its slip at the marina and headed toward Bimini. The boat's GPS, which was recovered, gave investigators an exact account of the vessel's movements. It provided a clear digital track from the moment the boat left until it was found abandoned and drifting the next day 140 miles south of its intended destination. The GPS showed that the boat was heading directly east for

THE CASE OF THE *JOE COOL* MURDERS

Bimini Bay. Near the end of the voyage, the GPS revealed that the boat behaved erratically, then stopped and drifted before turning south and going in a wobbly course until it ran out of fuel north of Cuba.

Calculating the speed of the boat and current, a Coast Guard GPS expert was able to determine the exact point in the ocean where the captain lost control of the boat. Shortly before 6 P.M. on Saturday, there was a period of one minute, eighteen seconds when the throttles had been cut back and no one was at the helm steering the boat. Nunez realized it was during this 78-second span that the four members of the *Joe Cool* were killed. The ocean at that location was about 1,000 feet deep, so the agent knew it would be virtually impossible to recover the murder weapons.

About three weeks after the high-seas murders, Miami-Dade police arrested Carlos Mulet, the owner of a shady auto repair shop in Hialeah. Mulet was charged with running a chop shop — a place where stolen cars are dismantled so their parts can be sold separately. He specialized in changing the appearance of stolen Mustang Cobras, which were then sold to willing buyers. After his arrest, Mulet cut a deal with prosecutors because he said he had information about the *Joe Cool* killings. He agreed to testify truthfully in court against Archer and Zarabozo in exchange for having the charges against him dropped.

The following week, Nunez grilled Mulet, who said that Zarabozo would hang around the shop because he loved fast cars and enjoyed going to the firing range nearby. Although he talked about wanting to be a cop, Zarabozo was short on ethics. Twice, the young man was paid $250 by Mulet for reporting the location of a parked Mustang Cobra — one that would then get stolen.

Mulet said he first met Archer when the suspect came to the shop to get his car repaired. Because Archer claimed to have some contacts high up in the government, Mulet befriended him, hoping Archer could fix the shop owner's traffic tickets. In March 2007 — six months before the murders — Archer asked Mulet for help in getting a gun. Mulet introduced him to Zarabozo, and the two hit it off because they both liked weapons and fast cars, and each had spent time in Cuba. Zarabozo acquired a gun, for which Archer paid him $400.

A short while later, according to Mulet, Archer said he needed help for "a big job." Mulet recommended Zarabozo, knowing the young man would be willing to break the law for the right price. The pair then began meeting at the shop, parking their cars out of range of the building's surveillance cameras.

Archer asked Mulet to teach him and Zarabozo how to walk into a local marina, sneak onto a dock, and steal a fast 60-foot boat that could handle heavy seas. Mulet, who once worked for a large boat-engine repair company in Miami, took the two men to several marinas to case out the vessels. It soon became clear to Mulet that the pair knew nothing about boats — including how to start one, never mind how to operate the sophisticated electronic gear or how to steer the big boat in open water.

"Guillermo [Zarabozo] told me he would make approximately one million dollars on this job," Mulet told Nunez. "Kirby [Archer] asked me to join them, but they didn't give me enough details, so I turned them down." Realizing that it was virtually impossible to steal a boat on their own, Archer told Mulet the pair would go to "Plan B" — hijack a charter fishing boat.

To confirm Mulet's story, investigators visited marinas from Key West to West Palm Beach and found surveillance video showing the three men checking out large, fast boats.

Because Cuba doesn't have a treaty with the United States to hand over fugitives, Nunez knew Archer wanted to get to the communist country and needed to hijack a boat to do so. "He had a passport but couldn't use it because of the warrant for his arrest," the agent told his team. "He was getting low on money. Where the heck was he going to go? Cuba is ninety miles across the water."

Investigators canvassed all the marinas in the area, and talked to charter boat captains who remembered Archer and Zarabozo offering to pay thousands of dollars for a trip to Bimini. But because the pair wanted to pay cash and declined to show their IDs or passports, the captains were suspicious and refused to take them.

THE CASE OF THE *JOE COOL* MURDERS

During the early phase of the investigation, Nunez and his team had gathered enough evidence for prosecutors to charge Archer and Zarabozo with kidnapping, murder, and other serious offenses, including seizing control of a ship by force. The crime was so evil that the government planned to pursue the death penalty for both of them.

Archer's attorney eventually approached the prosecutors with an offer that would save Archer from execution: The suspect would plead guilty to murder in exchange for a sentence of life in prison with no possibility of parole. The prosecution agreed to the deal. Most family members of the victims were grateful that they would be spared sitting through an agonizing trial, but some relatives wanted him tried, convicted, and put to death.

Nunez questioned Archer in prison several times, but every time, Archer changed his story slightly, so there was no way to know the real truth. Archer admitted that he killed Jake and Kelley Branam as part of the botched attempt to hijack the vessel. But he blamed Zarabozo for murdering the other two crewmen — and claimed that it was his friend's idea to shoot everyone and dump their bodies.

Archer said much of the evidence, including the clothes they wore during the killings, was thrown overboard. He said that once the boat ran out of fuel, they decided to take their chances on a life raft, hoping to get rescued by Cuban authorities.

When he arrived in court for sentencing in October 2008, Archer had a stone-faced expression. During the proceeding, he addressed the victims' loved ones. "For the family, I wish that, um, I wish I could take back what happened," he told them. "I wish I could show a little more emotion, but I'm not built that way."

Family members of the victims sobbed in court. "There's nothing I can say to fix it or take it back," Archer said. "I deserve to sit in jail the rest of my life. I deserve the death penalty, no question about that. I'm sorry what happened to them. These people were good people. They didn't do any wrong to me. They didn't deserve to die the way they did. But if it's any consolation, they didn't suffer much."

Sitting in the courtroom, Nunez winced when he heard the victims' relatives behind him weeping at the killer's cold-hearted words.

The judge sentenced Archer to five consecutive life terms in federal prison. *At least he will die in prison*, Nunez thought. *Will we ever know the truth for sure? No. Only the two killers know.*

Zarabozo refused to cut a similar deal with prosecutors and went to trial, facing 16 counts, including kidnapping and murder. Nunez felt confident the jury would convict the defendant, based on the hefty amount of circumstantial evidence against him.

In court, Zarabozo claimed Archer killed all four victims

and threatened to shoot him, too, if he didn't help clean up the murder scene.

To the shock of Nunez and the victims' families, the jurors were deadlocked on 12 of the most serious charges. Zarabozo was convicted on only four less serious counts of providing the gun used to kill the crew. The judge then declared a mistrial, which meant that Zarabozo would have to be tried all over again for kidnapping and murder.

When the verdict was read, Nunez shook his head in dismay. *This is so frustrating*, he thought. *We worked on this case day and night. And it was solid.* All it took was for one juror to vote opposite the others to cause a hung jury. Nunez figured that the juror was sympathetic toward Zarabozo because he was a young immigrant with no criminal record.

When the case went to the jury in the second trial in spring 2009, some of the victims' relatives feared another disappointing verdict. But Nunez was confident. He told them, "The jury is frustrated with him and his false testimony. They don't believe him. They're going to deliver a guilty verdict. I can feel it."

After deliberating for only a few hours, the jury returned to the courtroom. Their verdict: guilty on all counts of murder and kidnapping.

A wave of relief swept over Nunez. He thought about all the time and effort he and his team had put into this case — his fellow agents, the lab techs, investigators from the Coast

Guard; Miami-Dade Police Department; Broward Sheriff's Office; Alcohol, Tobacco, and Firearms; Florida Department of Law Enforcement; Arkansas State Police; and United States Attorney's Office.

Nunez thought about all the days that ended in the wee hours of the night, the dinners that were missed, the leads that went nowhere, the thousands of questions that were asked, the lies that were sifted from facts. For 18 long months, he lived and breathed the *Joe Cool* murders and gave the case everything he had. And it had all paid off because two killers will remain locked in prison forever.

Now, as he sat in the courtroom looking at the jubilation on the faces of the victims' emotional loved ones, Nunez thought, *This is one of the greatest days of my life.*

During his sentencing hearing, Zarabozo told the victims' families, "I'm really sorry for the loss of your family members. But I had nothing to do with it. When I got on that boat, I didn't know what Archer was going to do. I'm a victim of Archer, too."

Declaring Zarabozo's story was all lies, the judge sentenced him to five life sentences for the murders and conspiracy, plus 85 more years for a dozen other charges.

THE CASE OF THE POISONED SWEETS

Rat poison?" said Special Agent Monica Patton, repeating what the technician at the FBI Laboratory had just informed her over the phone. Patton had never dealt with a case quite as bizarre as this one.

It was spring 2005. Threatening letters — each with a different return address and signature — had been sent to all nine U.S. Supreme Court justices, FBI Director Robert Mueller, FBI Deputy Director John Pistole, and the chiefs of staff of the army, navy, and air force. All 14 envelopes contained either a home-baked cookie or piece of candy taped to a typewritten one-page note that said "We are" or "I am" followed by "going to kill you. This is poisoned."

On the phone, the lab technician explained to Patton, "The cookies and candy were laced with *bromadiolone rodenticide,* a fancy name for rat poison. It came in pellet form in the cookies. When baked, the poisonous elements got released in the cookies, so it wasn't easily detectable."

Patton wondered, *Is this a sick joke? A test of our security by terrorists? The work of a deranged person? A warning from an antigovernment group?*

As the threat coordinator for FBI investigations of crimes against the Supreme Court, members of Congress, and other government officials, Patton was determined to solve the perplexing case quickly.

Still fresh in her mind were the deadly 2001 anthrax attacks. Letters containing lethal spores of the bacteria anthrax had been mailed to several news media outlets and the offices of two United States senators, killing five people and infecting 17 others. In that case, the FBI concluded a rogue government scientist, who died before he could be arrested, had been the perpetrator.

Ever since the anthrax scare, all mail sent to the Supreme Court justices and other top government officials are carefully screened by the U.S. Postal Inspection Service. Most envelopes are run through rollers, which tend to flatten anything inside them. That's what happened to the 14 suspect envelopes. After getting crushed by the rollers, pieces of the cookies and candy seeped out. This alerted mail handlers, who intercepted the envelopes and immediately tested them for biological, chemical, or nuclear threats.

THE CASE OF THE POISONED SWEETS

The tests ruled out any of those concerns, so the menacing notes were put in a special clear sealed pouch and turned over to Patton. Before looking at them in her office, she put on latex gloves so she wouldn't contaminate them. Resting on her desk was a little magnifying glass, a prize that she had plucked out of a Cheerios box a few years earlier. She picked it up and used it to examine the notes. Some of them contained small blotches of a smeared greenish substance, which later turned out to be the rat poison. The typewritten words seemed to have similar characteristics, which meant they could have come from the same typewriter. All the signatures, though, had different handwriting.

She glanced at the words *going to kill you. This person is very angry and frustrated*, Patton thought.

The agent, who had spent most of her ten years at the Bureau investigating violent crimes, grew increasingly concerned about the safety of the justices and the others, including her boss, the FBI director. She needed to find the origin of the letters before the person or persons tried to strike again.

Patton hand-delivered the notes and envelopes to the FBI Laboratory in Quantico, Virginia, for detailed analysis. She told the lab technicians this was a priority case. She needed to have every possible test done to these letters, including the search for DNA; latent fingerprints; and trace evidence, like a strand of hair, skin cells, and microscopic fibers of clothing or carpeting; as well as document examinations, including analysis of the typing and signatures. She knew it would take time because the lab had to go through a thoughtful, methodical process in a certain order so that one test didn't adversely affect another test. The agent felt confident the lab technicians would turn up something.

Meanwhile, Patton and her team focused on the different names on the return addresses. Some of the letters were postmarked from New York City even though there were return addresses from Connecticut; New Jersey; Washington, D.C.; Maryland; Florida; Georgia; Illinois; and Missouri.

Patton sent special agents to all the addresses to question the alleged senders. Everyone who was interviewed denied sending the letters and claimed they didn't know who else could have done it. Background checks showed they were upstanding citizens. All voiced their surprise and dismay that someone or some group had used their names and addresses to frame them.

It looked like the investigation was heading toward a dead end. But a blind alley like this just motivates many FBI agents to work even harder. It did for Monica Patton.

She reminded herself to be creative because criminals are creative, so she tried to think outside the box. *Sometimes people say things that mean very little to them but are greatly significant to the FBI during an investigation*, she thought. *Maybe there is some common thread that links all the names together.*

THE CASE OF THE POISONED SWEETS

Special Agent David Brown from the Jacksonville, Florida, office called and said he had interviewed a woman in Tampa whose name was on the return address of one of the letters. "She's very upset over this," he told Patton. "She claims she didn't send it."

"Could she be lying?" Patton asked.

"Given the background check I did on her, I'm pretty sure she's telling the truth. So where do we go from here?"

Patton and Brown then worked up a new approach. "What if you go back to her and show her the entire list of names on the return addresses," Patton told him. "Maybe she'll see something in common. Do you think it would be safe to let her see it?"

"She definitely seems the type who would be comfortable cooperating with the FBI," Brown said. "Let me try."

Two hours later, Brown called Patton and said, "You're not going to believe this. I showed her the list of names, and she physically went pale. She looked stunned and was speechless. She said, 'Many of these are members of my sorority from 1967 at Stetson University.'

"I asked her, 'Who would have sent a letter like this? Did you have anyone in your sorority who was angry or more vocal than the rest? Someone with mental problems? Someone who was frustrated?' She came up with the name Bobbie March. She said Bobbie was troubled and hadn't had it easy in life. It's someone we might want to look at."

THE CASE OF THE POISONED SWEETS

Patton then called the special agents at other field offices and told them to go back to the people they had interviewed, show them the list of names, and ask them if they had any thoughts on who could have sent the threatening notes. When the agents reported back to Patton, she learned that half the persons mentioned the same name — Bobbie March.

It was the first big break in the case.

Using all the criminal databases available to the FBI, Patton ran a background check on March. The security staffs for the Supreme Court, the U.S. Postal Service, and the Capitol police were also doing the same thing. The information that Patton was finding proved unsettling. Bobbie March — whose real name was Barbara Joan March — had a history of using poison and engaging in violent behavior.

She had been in and out of prison nine times in the previous 20 years in Connecticut. In 1985, her brother, Richard March, contacted U.S. postal inspectors and turned over a bottle of wine that had been mailed to his and Barbara's 65-year-old mother, Elaine. He became suspicious after noticing the seal was broken on the bottle. Tests by the state toxicology laboratory determined the wine was laced with the allergy medicine Benadryl, which, if mixed with alcohol, could have been lethal if consumed. Similar bottles of poisoned wine had been sent to other relatives as well. Investigators also found rat poison among Barbara March's belongings at that time. Two years later, she was convicted of attempted murder after shooting at Richard and his wife,

Diane, outside their home in Stratford, Connecticut. Although Richard wasn't injured, one bullet struck Diane in the chest, but she survived. After serving time in prison, March appeared to stay out of trouble.

The more Patton learned about the suspect, the more the agent was concerned that the FBI was dealing with an unstable, volatile person.

New investigations by agents turned up even more evidence that pointed to March. In addition to the former sorority sisters, the remaining seven persons whose names were on the return addresses also had a direct link to her. Three had attended elementary or high school with her, one was a former coworker, another lived with her while the two studied abroad in Spain, one lived with her brother, and another had the same name as her former husband.

Patton felt confident that the case was heading in the right direction. But she didn't want to ignore any other possibilities, knowing that such thinking can cripple an investigation. *Keep an open mind,* the agent reminded herself. *There's always the chance that she isn't working alone. Is she part of a dangerous network or a domestic terrorist group?*

The FBI Lab reported that it could not find any usable DNA on the letters or any fingerprints. But even that disappointing news told Patton something. *It says that this person is someone who had thought out the entire scheme, put some real planning into it, and used gloves. We are dealing with someone who is quite clever and potentially more dangerous.*

The lab did manage to recover numerous clothing fibers from the tape that was used to seal the envelopes and to affix the cookies and candy to the letters. Patton was told these hard-to-see fibers likely came off the culprit's clothing during the preparation of the death threats. Among the fibers that were found were those that came from a red cotton shirt, a pink-and-blue cotton shirt, a pink furry sweater, and a red sweater.

There was one other important finding. The lab determined that the letters were all written on the same kind of electric typewriter — a Panasonic. There were certain similar characteristics in the typing — the way the letters *A*, *J*, and *Y* were slightly askew, the way the letters struck the paper, the way the spacing was spread between the letters. The notes all shared those same distinguishing traits.

However, none of the laboratory tests connected March directly to the crime — yet. But Patton considered her the prime suspect. It was time to search the woman's residence.

By now, the FBI knew that March, a petite woman in her late fifties, worked at a fast-food restaurant in Bridgeport, Connecticut. She lived in a tiny rented single-room apartment in a large brick building called Prospect House, although she sometimes stayed elsewhere with friends or relatives. Prospect House was a residence for people who had been recently released from prison or were recovering from drug, alcohol, or mental problems and needed a place to live while they tried to reenter society.

Patton arrived in Bridgeport and teamed up with Special Agent Michael Syrax and the FBI's Evidence Response Team. Armed with a search warrant, the agents talked to the Prospect House director, who told them that March had never caused a moment of trouble. The director took the agents to the suspect's unoccupied apartment and opened the door.

Before entering, everyone, including Patton, donned Tyvek suits, full-body disposable protective gear, because they didn't want to contaminate the room during their search. The stifling summer heat made wearing the Tyvek suit uncomfortably hot, but Patton didn't mind, not after she and her team stepped into the room and found a wealth of evidence. Sitting on the counter were bags of sugary treats and jars of candy. The agent noticed that some of the sweets resembled the candy that had been attached to the threatening notes. Patton, who had a sweet tooth, saw a bag of her favorite mints and wished the situation would have been different so she could have eaten some, if not all, of them.

What surprised the agents the most were all the lists they found scattered throughout the room. Patton looked at a list that had first names with numbers 1 to 14 next to them. Several had an initial after them and all had a name of a state. "I recognize these first names," Patton told her colleagues. "Each one is a name on a return address of the fourteen threatening letters." Patton quickly figured out that the initials next to the first names referred to their last names, and the states referred to where each person lived.

Adding to the mounting evidence against March, the agents found several revealing to-do lists. One included an alarming item: "Have a plan to get a gun." A different, much longer list had such entries as "find people," "phone books," "U.S. Search," "lease a car," "a route and a plan," "type letters," "candy and tape — no fingerprints — use gloves."

In addition, Patton and her team found numerous maps printed from Internet websites. Someone had handwritten circles where prominent people — including some Supreme Court justices — lived. Other maps bore the addresses of those persons who supposedly had mailed the letters. The agents also discovered pieces of paper containing references to expenses for candy, paper, and envelopes.

With a list prepared by the lab technicians of specific clothes to seize, Patton carefully went through March's closet and pulled out things that likely contained the identical fibers found on the letters. Among the apparel that the agent took were a red cotton shirt, a pink-and-blue cotton shirt, a pink furry sweater, and a red sweater.

But one of the items she most wanted to find — the Panasonic on which the letters had been typed — wasn't in the room.

Once all the evidence was collected and sealed in special plastic bags, Patton asked the Prospect House director if the office had a typewriter. "We don't use one," the director said. "In fact, we don't have one at the facility."

As Patton left the old brownstone building, she wondered, *Where would March have typed those letters?* The agent spent a moment pondering the question. She knew many of the residents were either ex-cons or were out on bond awaiting trial. She also knew that defendants often typed up their own letters to the court.

Seeing a grizzled, tipsy man leaning against the wall of Prospect House, she asked, "Do you live here?"

"Yeah," he replied warily.

"We're not here to cause you any trouble," said Patton, who had a knack for getting people to open up to her. "Would you help me out, please?"

"Well, um, all right."

"Where would you go to type a letter around here?"

"Bridgeport Public Library. It's about a ten-minute walk from here. They have typewriters that people can use."

That would be a logical place where March could type her letters, Patton thought.

She and Syrax drove straight to the library. There, the head librarian showed them three typewriters that were available to members of the public. All three were electric Panasonics — the same brand and model that the FBI Lab said had been used to type the threatening notes. Patton scanned the sign-up sheets that recorded the names of users of the typewriters. Bobbie March's name was on one of the sheets.

THE CASE OF THE POISONED SWEETS

If the FBI could confirm that the letters came from a specific typewriter, it would be further proof that March was the perpetrator. The only way to know for sure was to compare microscopic fibers from the ribbons with those found on the letters. For that, the agents needed to secure a subpoena, which they did.

When Patton and Syrax returned to the library, they were dressed casually without FBI insignias because they didn't want to alarm the patrons. Using sheets of blank paper, the agents sat down at each typewriter and typed every single letter of the alphabet, both upper and lower case, at various pressures from lightly tapping the keys to almost banging on them. They typed each number and symbol, hit the shift keys and return handle, and changed spacing. After photographing the front and back of each machine and recording the serial numbers, the agents carefully packaged the ribbons and the typed pages and sealed them. Because the agents felt bad about taking the ribbons, they went to an office supply store and replaced them so patrons could continue using the typewriters.

The seized ribbons were sent to the FBI Lab's Questioned Document Unit, where technician Hector Gonzalez created a special exam just for this case. Each typewriter had its own unique characteristics and impressions. He was able to analyze the pages that the agents had typed and compared the residue from the typewriter ribbons on the threatening notes. By identifying specific impressions, he narrowed it down to one of the Bridgeport Library's typewriters.

Meanwhile, other lab technicians had matched up the fibers found on the threatening notes to fibers in the clothes that Patton had taken from March's closet.

There was now enough probable cause for Patton to obtain an arrest warrant for Barbara March. Because Patton had returned to Washington, D.C., it was up to Syrax to bring in the suspect. Knowing March had a history of violence — after all, she had shot at her own brother and sister-in-law — Syrax returned to Prospect House accompanied by a small SWAT team. Fortunately, March did not resist or cause a scene when she was arrested in her room.

Syrax phoned Patton and reported, "We have her in custody. She came peaceably."

"That's a great sense of relief," said Patton. "It feels good to take a person like this off the street, especially someone who threatened the Supreme Court justices and our director."

March was soon whisked to Washington for her initial appearance in federal court. Patton was there to see her for the first time, trying to get an impression of the suspect and study her mannerisms, reactions, and personality. March's hair was dyed black, which contrasted sharply with her pale skin. Her thin, arching eyebrows framed dark troubled eyes. Patton couldn't help but notice that the woman's bloodred lipstick was put on slightly crooked.

THE CASE OF THE POISONED SWEETS

Later, the agent met March face-to-face when the suspect, under court order, had to give handwriting samples. During much of the session, March locked her eyes in a silent, angry stare at Patton. *She strikes me as someone who's so tightly wound that there's something scary going on inside her head*, the agent thought. *I don't know what it is, but it's dangerous.*

At one point, when March was told to write with her opposite hand, she asked Patton, "Do you have a family?"

The agent wasn't about to give her any personal information, not even that she was a working mom. Leaning across the table, Patton replied curtly, "Just do as you're instructed."

March glowered at her. To Patton, the suspect looked at her as if the agent was the most hated person on earth, and given the opportunity, would be on the woman's next death-threat list.

During the post-arrest investigation, Patton tried to establish March's motive for the poisoned letters. Field agents reinterviewed the suspect's former friends and colleagues whom she had tried to frame. The FBI learned that at various times throughout her life, she became angry with each person for different reasons. The issues were usually over something that seemed trivial to them, but not to March. She held a grudge against these people and wanted revenge.

So in her disturbed mind, she thought the best way to get even was to get them in trouble with the law. She hoped to do that by putting their names and addresses on the threatening notes that accompanied the poisoned treats and on the envelopes. March's actions, Patton was convinced, had nothing to do with politics or any Supreme Court decision or hostility toward the military or FBI. The crime was spurred strictly by misplaced anger toward people who in the defendant's mind somehow had abandoned or wronged her.

In follow-up FBI interviews, these persons believed that March was suffering from mental issues. Some felt bad for her; others wanted her locked up for life.

A few months after the arrest, Patton visited the Supreme Court, where she shook hands with Justice Antonin Scalia. As an American history buff whose grandfather once argued here, the agent stood in wonder inside the imposing, marble-lined court chamber. She gazed at the twenty-four soaring columns, nine high-backed leather chairs, and the raised mahogany bench. She thought about all the landmark decisions that were made in this hallowed building, decisions that in many cases changed the lives of millions of Americans and altered the course of history.

As Monica Patton continued to revel inside this magnificent chamber, she realized the importance of it all — and how vital it was that the Supreme Court justices and the public stay safe. *Being here just reaffirmed why I do my job,* she thought. *This is why we worked so hard to solve this case.*

THE CASE OF THE POISONED SWEETS

* * *

On March 14, 2006 — nearly a year after her arrest — Barbara Joan March, 60, pleaded guilty to 14 counts of mailing injurious articles. She was later sentenced to 15 years in federal prison.

Her sentence would have been much less had she sent the letters to most anyone else. But in her misguided attempt to cause more harm to the alleged senders, she had chosen to mail the threatening letters to high-level federal officials. Targeting them tacked on about five years to her punishment.

THE COLD CASE OF
JENNIFER SCHUETT

Afraid of the dark, eight-year-old Jennifer Schuett always slept with her single mom. But on the night of August 10, 1990, chigger bites caused the girl to toss and turn and scratch so much that her mother made her go to her own room down the hall.

Jennifer read and then counted coins in her piggy bank before falling asleep with the light on. The curtains were partially drawn over the closed first-floor window overlooking the parking lot of the Yorktown Apartments in Dickinson, Texas.

Sometime between midnight and 2 A.M., Jennifer awoke in the arms of a strange man carrying her to his car. She couldn't breathe or scream because his hand covered her mouth and nose. He told the terrified girl that he was an undercover police officer, but she didn't believe him.

Moments later he held a knife to her in the front seat of the car. He snarled, "Are you scared, little girl? Am I scaring you?"

They drove through residential areas, past her grandparents' house and Silbernagel Elementary School, where she was looking forward to starting third grade. Softening his tone, the man offered her candy, but she refused because she had been taught never to take candy from strangers. Then he drove to a nearby weed-infested empty lot and choked her until she lost consciousness.

When Jennifer regained her senses, she felt burrs and thorns scratching her back as she was being dragged by her feet. Her throat had been slashed. With remarkable presence of mind, Jennifer figured her attacker thought she was dead, so she closed her eyes and remained motionless. After he released his grip on her, she heard him walk to his car and drive off, leaving her to die. Then she passed out.

Jennifer woke up later that morning, too weak to move because she was slowly bleeding to death. She tried to scream, but no sound came out. She didn't realize that her voice box had been damaged during the assault. She could see passing cars through the weeds, but no one could see her.

Late in the day, about 14 hours after she had been snatched from her bedroom, Jennifer heard children playing hide-and-seek and then felt something touch her foot. It was a classmate gently kicking her to see if she was alive.

Within minutes, a police officer arrived and told her, "Stay with me. Everything is going to be okay." A helicopter flew her to University of Texas Medical Branch at Galveston, where doctors inserted a breathing tube and saved her life.

A few days later, when Jennifer was strong enough, the police began questioning her. Unable to talk, she blinked once for "yes" and twice for "no." She also scribbled her answers on a little note pad. She described the suspect as a white male, in his twenties, with dark hair and "yucky" teeth. He was sloppy, wore a white T-shirt, and drove an old, dented blue car with beer cans scattered on the floor. One other thing: He told her his name was Dennis.

Despite being mute, Jennifer managed to describe the suspect's facial features to a police artist, who drew a composite picture that was given to the news media. Shocked by the brutality of the attack, the citizens of Dickinson locked their doors for the first time and warily eyed the town's shady characters, wondering if one of them was the assailant.

Although doctors said she would never speak again, Jennifer regained her voice within a few weeks. But she needed months of medical treatment and rehabilitation before she could return to school. She and her mother were so traumatized that they moved out of their apartment to live with her grandparents two miles away.

Meanwhile, police in Dickinson tried desperately to find the attacker. The only good physical evidence was a man's T-shirt and Jennifer's pajama top and shorts that were recovered from a ditch a few blocks away from where the girl was found. But there wasn't a scientific test sophisticated enough to identify the microscopic amounts of DNA on the items. Police ran down more than 200 leads, but came up empty-handed. Weeks turned into months, months into years.

Jennifer grew up and went to college. Not a day went by that she didn't think about that horrendous assault on her life. She kept prodding the police to keep looking for the monster. But with each passing year, the case grew colder and colder. The files were handed down from one detective to another until . . .

FBI Special Agent Richard "Rich" Rennison was at his desk in League City, Texas, on a March day in 2008 when, out of the blue, he received a call from Dickinson Police Detective Tim Cromie. Over the years, the two had teamed up together on several investigations and had formed a solid working relationship.

"I got assigned the Jennifer Schuett cold case," said Cromie, who then gave the agent a brief rundown of the crime. "I just met with her, and she's very upset because the case has been languishing for eighteen years. It's gone through four detectives. She was crying and said, 'Is anyone ever going to do anything?' I told her, 'I'm going to do something. I'm going to call in the FBI. They have so many more resources than we do.' So, Rich, will you work with me on this case?"

"Count me in," replied Rennison, a nine-year veteran in the Bureau who previously was a police officer with experience solving crimes against children. Even though he had an eight-year-old daughter who was the same age now that Jennifer was when she was victimized, the agent didn't need any extra motivation to try and hunt down the offender. It was his job, his mission — a challenge he relished.

When Rennison arrived at the Dickinson Police Department, he and Cromie went through the box that contained all the files on the case. They examined the 27 handwritten notes that Jennifer had written during her hospitalization when she wasn't able to speak. Seeing one of her notes that said her assailant mentioned his name was Dennis, the agent thought, *There's only a ten percent chance he used his real name. Who would be that dumb? I don't want to be looking only for someone named Dennis.*

"There are so many studies that show victims of a traumatic assault have a very poor recollection of actually describing things accurately," Rennison told Cromie. "I don't want to rely one hundred percent on her notes. But I don't want to discount them, either."

Looking at photos of Jennifer taken at the hospital right after the brutal attack, Rennison said, "How she survived is unbelievable. It just wasn't her time."

The two men agreed not to talk to the previous investigators who had handled her case because the pair didn't want to get influenced by the others' thoughts and beliefs. "We need to come in with a fresh set of eyes and be as objective as we can and follow the physical evidence," Rennison said. "It's easy to follow another investigator's suspicions, but they don't necessarily lead you to the perpetrator."

The pair went to the Galveston County Sheriff's Office's evidence room, where the clothes that had been found near the crime scene had been preserved and stored. Rennison believed that the latest scientific advances in DNA testing, which weren't available in 1990, might now reveal the attacker's identity. So the agent sent the clothes to the FBI Laboratory in Quantico, Virginia, for testing. Because of an enormous backlog of samples from other crimes, he was told it could take up to a year before he would learn the results. There was no guarantee that any DNA would be found. And even if it was found, there was always the possibility that no match would show up in the FBI's vast nationwide database of offenders' DNA.

Later that day, Cromie introduced Rennison to Jennifer, a 26-year-old woman who still lived in the area. The agent tried to reassure her that they would do everything they could to capture her attacker. "I know Tim, and we work well together," he told her. "We have a big interest in this case. It's not our only one; we have many others. But I promise you that we will work this until there's nothing left to be worked."

"I've thought of him every single day," she said. "I will never give up until he is found and brought to justice. I don't know who he is or where he lives, but in my heart, I know he's out there either in prison or living a lie."

Throughout the next few months, Rennison and Cromie examined old records and documents, searching for clues. Making things more difficult, some records from 1990 had been lost or destroyed.

A folder in the original investigation had a list of all the residents who lived in the apartment complex at the time, so Rennison ran the criminal histories on each person to see if anyone had been involved in a crime against a child. The agent and Cromie reinterviewed dozens of people, hoping to find someone who might have been afraid to talk to police back in 1990, but would be willing to come forward now.

Rennison doubted this was the first time the suspect had committed this type of crime. He compared specifics of the case with other abductions, but none seemed to have the same MO, or *modus operandi*, meaning the criminal's method of operation.

In summer 2009, Rennison received an email from Tamyra Moretti, the FBI lab technician who was trying to find DNA on the clothes that she could match to a name. She wrote: "The first round of DNA testing has been conducted. Unfortunately, there's not enough DNA to make a comparable profile. At this point, testing would normally stop. However, I feel we can get better results if I try again using different methods, so stand by and I'll get back to you in several weeks."

The news was somewhat deflating to Rennison, but he still held out hope. A few weeks later, Moretti called him and reported, "The second round didn't go any better than the first, but I'm going to try one more thing."

Rennison sighed. "It looks like another swing and a miss. We'll have to focus on all the other avenues." When he first submitted the evidence to the lab, he was confident of a DNA match. But he was feeling much less so now.

He and Cromie decided to appeal to the public, hoping to draw out someone who was close to the offender, such as an ex-wife or ex-girlfriend. Special Agent Shauna Dunlap of the FBI office in Houston launched a media campaign and announced a $10,000 reward for information leading to the arrest and conviction of Jennifer's attacker. She arranged for Jennifer to do interviews with CNN and local TV and to tell her story on the popular TV show *America's Most Wanted*.

"I hope one day to see my attacker convicted," Jennifer told reporters. "I want to look him in the face in the courtroom and let him see he didn't win. He messed with the wrong girl. I want him to pay for what he did, and I don't want him to hurt anyone else. If he's not in jail, he's still out there committing crimes against children, and that's what breaks my heart."

The media blitz brought a few new leads, but nothing panned out.

During the investigation, Rennison and Cromie learned about a guy named Kenny, who supposedly told his girlfriend during an argument, "If you don't do what I tell you, you're going to end up like what I did to that little girl Jennifer."

Turning their focus on Kenny, the agent and detective learned that he had grown up close to where Jennifer lived, he knew her mother, and he was currently in prison for attacking a child. Not only that, but his mug shot had a strong resemblance to the police artist's sketch of Jennifer's attacker.

Rennison and Cromie planned to visit him in prison once the agent returned from Washington, D.C., where he was attending a training seminar.

Rennison was asleep in his hotel room on September 22 when he was jarred awake around 2:30 A.M. by the ringing of his cell phone. He didn't get to it in time. Squinting through his bleary eyes, he bolted up when he saw who the caller was: Tamyra Moretti. *Oh my goodness! She wouldn't be calling me at this hour unless she had some news*, he thought.

The agent immediately called her back and asked, "Did you find anything?"

"We've got a hit," she announced. "We've got a solid match. It's guaranteed."

"Who is it?" asked Rennison, expecting to hear that the DNA belonged to Kenny.

"Dennis Earl Bradford."

"Huh? Who is that? I never heard his name ever come up in our investigation."

"He was convicted of kidnapping a woman in Hot Springs, Arkansas, in 1996."

"Arkansas?" *Nothing is making sense to me*, he thought. *I'm beginning to wonder if there's a chance of a mistake.*

Moretti assured the agent that the DNA on the clothes found near the crime scene definitely matched Bradford's DNA. She added that Bradford served four years of a twelve-year prison sentence before he was released.

Seconds after hanging up with the lab technician, Rennison called Cromie and woke him up with the good news: "Tim, we got a hit!"

"So who is it?"

"Dennis Earl Bradford, a convicted kidnapper in Arkansas."

"I never heard of him. Are you sure?"

Neither Cromie nor Rennison went back to sleep that night. They were too pumped about the possibility that after all these years, they finally had the name of a prime suspect. On his laptop, the agent tapped into some of the FBI databases and found that Bradford had indeed lived in Texas back in the early 1990s. That got rid of any thoughts that the lab had made an error.

Early the next morning, Cromie began a thorough background check of Bradford. The detective found that Bradford had attended Dickinson High School. In 1987, the suspect was cited for a traffic ticket and gave his home address, which was only a quarter mile from Jennifer's apartment.

In 1991, six months after Jennifer had been attacked, Bradford was arrested in Arkansas for assaulting a woman at night inside a post office. For some unknown reason, there was no record of a conviction in that case. Five years later, Bradford was arrested and convicted of kidnapping a 35-year-old woman he had met at a Hot Springs nightclub. While holding her captive, he had cut her neck with a knife, but the wound wasn't nearly as severe as Jennifer's. It was this conviction that put Bradford's DNA into the system and ultimately led to a match.

The investigators learned that the suspect was working as a welder in North Little Rock, Arkansas. He was married with two children and three stepchildren. Rennison arranged for FBI agents in Little Rock to keep Bradford under constant surveillance while the case was built against him.

Back in Texas, Rennison and Cromie set out to prove Bradford was in Dickinson at the time of Jennifer's kidnapping. Nothing much stood out about Bradford in his younger days. He was a rather quiet, unassuming student in high school. Aside from a few traffic tickets, he appeared not to be in trouble with the law.

The agent and detective had to walk a fine line when interviewing people who knew Bradford back then. The investigators withheld as much information as they could to prevent the possibility that any friends or relatives would tip him off that he was a prime suspect.

It took a week for the Texas Division of Motor Vehicles to email Rennison Bradford's Texas driver's license picture from 1990. When the agent opened the email and saw the photo, he was stunned. The picture had an uncanny resemblance to the police composite drawing made from the description that Jennifer had given from her hospital bed. Rennison could hardly believe that a traumatized little girl who couldn't talk was able to give such an accurate description of her attacker by scribbling notes. And yet there it was on his computer screen.

When Cromie saw Bradford's 1990 photo, he, too, was amazed, telling Rennison, "The police sketch looks like it had been drawn directly from the photo."

With the information they had compiled, the investigators were poised to close in on Bradford, who had no clue that his life as a free man was coming to an end. They flew to North Little Rock and put together a team that included other FBI agents and local police.

Because Rennison and Cromie wanted to get a confession out of Bradford after his arrest, they needed to know more about the suspect as a person. So the agent called in members of the FBI's Behavioral Analysis Unit

(BAU), a specially trained team that develops psychological profiles of people. These profiles help authorities choose the right approach when they are interrogating suspects.

To gather facts about Bradford, the BAU team decided to interview some of his neighbors. As luck would have it, one neighbor was a cop and the other was a fire chief. For more than two hours, the team asked questions about the suspect. When the session was over, Rennison and Cromie knew more about Bradford than many of his own friends. The investigators learned that his most prized possession was his dog, Nacho; that he loved his cast-iron pots; that he wouldn't respond well if authorities got in his face and yelled at him.

The plan to arrest Bradford called for a patrolman to pull him over for a traffic violation on his way to work early the next morning, October 13. The cop would then inform him, "Sir, I see we have an outstanding warrant for your arrest. I'm not sure what it's for, probably some traffic violation. I'll have to take you to the police station so we can sort this out." There would be no mention of kidnapping or attempted murder. The investigators didn't want Bradford to have any time to think about how he was going to answer their questions about Jennifer.

The arrest came off without a hitch, exactly as planned. When Bradford was brought to the police station, Rennison and Cromie were waiting for him. At first, they talked to him about everything but the case. Finally, it was time to confront Bradford.

"Have you ever heard the name Jennifer Schuett?" Rennison asked him.

The suspect's eyes grew wide in surprise. "Yes," he replied.

"What do you know about her personally?"

"Personally? I don't know anything about her."

"Did you have an occasion to come in contact with her?"

Bradford hung his head and mumbled, "Yes."

"Tell me about it."

"No."

"Why won't you tell me?"

"You've done your homework. You know."

I think he's going to give it up, the agent thought. *I think he's going to confess.* But Bradford refused to admit he attacked her. For the first couple of hours of the interrogation, he danced around the subject. Showing little remorse, and upset that he had been caught, he sidestepped tough questions and offered vague answers.

After three hours of calm but persistent prodding by the investigators, Bradford began to wear down. His nerves were frayed, his body tense. Grudgingly, he divulged little bits and pieces of information about that night. He admitted that Jennifer was in the car with him, but he still wouldn't say that he had attacked her.

Following a long silence, Rennison told him, "Dennis, if you could see her today, you'd be proud of her."

Bradford, who had been staring blankly at the floor, looked up and burst into tears. "Oh my God, she's alive?" he cried out. "She's alive?" The pressure from all the years of hiding that terrible secret, storing the pent-up guilt, and stifling the truth had finally exploded in an emotional torrent.

He confirmed everything that Jennifer had originally told authorities about the kidnapping. He even added details that she hadn't recalled. Listening to Bradford's account, Rennison was dumbstruck at how accurate Jennifer had been. *Oh my goodness, I can't believe an eight-year-old girl who went through this horrible thing was so accurate.*

But it was still a challenge to get a full confession out of him. "At some point she got cut," Rennison said. "Tell me about that."

Bradford was silent for a long time before he mumbled, "I did that. You got me."

"Where did she get cut?" the agent asked.

"On her throat."

"Are you ready to admit everything?"

"I can't bring myself to say it."

"Let's hear you say it, Dennis."

"There is not a day that goes by, not a single day, that I don't see that baby," blurted Bradford in a voice cracking with emotion. "I took that little girl out of the window. She was freaking out. She was crying for her mother. I told her everything was going to be all right. I dragged her in the field and I attacked her. She was an innocent . . . and I was a sick, deranged, beat-up, little punk. I had strangled her to the point of unconsciousness . . . and I cut her throat."

There! He finally said it. We have a confession.

"Dennis, why Jennifer? Why did you choose her as your victim?"

"I don't know. I was just driving around. I had some cousins who lived in her apartment complex, so I pulled into the parking lot and walked around. I saw something in that window — I don't remember what it was, balloons maybe — that made me think it was a girl's room. The light was on. Even though the curtains were closed, there was a little gap that I could see through." Bradford shook his head in resignation and added, "I knew what I was going to do, but I didn't know why."

This was a random attack? Rennison didn't believe it. *What are the odds that the one night that Jennifer was sleeping alone with the light on would be the one night that Bradford was looking for a victim?* (Try as they might, investigators could never find any evidence that Bradford knew Jennifer, her mother or father, or even their friends and relatives prior to the crime. It appeared to be a random act of violence.)

Rennison and Cromie escorted a handcuffed Bradford back to Texas on a commercial airliner. He was cordial, respectful, and polite during the flight. When he was brought to the police station in Dickinson, the place was swarming with reporters, photographers, and TV crews.

While Bradford was being processed, Jennifer spoke at a highly emotional press conference. "This event in my life was a tragic one, but today, nineteen years later, I stand here and want you all to know that I am okay," she said, fighting back tears. "I am not a victim, but instead, victorious. I hope that I can be an example to others — you can have the strength to fight back. You can get justice, no matter how long it takes."

She gave special thanks to Rennison and Cromie, saying, "They promised me that they were not going to stop until they solved the case. And they kept their promise."

After Bradford was booked, he was placed in a room with a two-way mirror so he couldn't see out, but others could see in. Standing behind the mirror in the adjoining room was Jennifer. Loved ones who accompanied her were crying because the man who assaulted her had finally, after all these years, been captured. Rennison was in the room, too, and noticed that Jennifer stared at Bradford without any hatred in her eyes — just curiosity. "I finally get to see the man who did this to me," she murmured.

Although they were physically and emotionally spent, Rennison and Cromie went out to a late dinner with Jennifer and her fiancé, Jonathan Martinez, to celebrate Bradford's capture. As everyone clinked glasses, Cromie said to her, "Rich and I told you we'd get him."

Bradford was charged with kidnapping and attempted murder and held in the Galveston County Jail under $1 million bail. Before Jennifer had a chance to testify against him in court, he hanged himself in his cell on May 10, 2010.

"I looked forward to facing him in the courtroom, but I was robbed of that opportunity," Jennifer said in a statement. "I feel very blessed and grateful that I was able to find out who attacked me all of those years ago, and that he was arrested, and taken off of the streets so that he couldn't harm anyone else. I will continue to use my voice and advocate for other victims of crime."

In November 2012, Jennifer gave birth to her first child, a daughter named Jenna. Jennifer continues to speak out on behalf of victims' rights.

THE CASE OF THE FRIDAY NIGHT BANK ROBBER

With several law enforcement officers at his side, Special Agent Raymond Carr studied a bizarre mix of items spread out on a table at the police station in Radnor, Pennsylvania: two ski masks, eight Halloween masks, five handguns, about 500 rounds of ammunition, food rations, books, maps, newspaper articles, and hand-written notes regarding 160 banks in the Northeast.

The day before, on April 1, 2001, two thirteen-year-old boys were building a fort in the woods across the street from the station when they spotted two three-foot-long PVC pipes, each capped at both ends, inside a plastic drainage pipe. They opened up the pipes and found newspaper clippings of bank robberies and a page of instructions on how to clean a Beretta, a type of handgun. The boys alerted the police, who returned to the site where they discovered a hidden, carefully constructed, three-by-four-foot military-style bunker lined in brick and cement blocks. It was neatly filled with PVC pipes and waterproof containers holding the items that Carr was now examining.

"Do you think it's from some extremist group planning an assault?" an officer asked Carr.

"I don't know," the agent replied. His eyes remained focused on the detailed list of the banks and their addresses in small towns stretching from Upstate New York and Connecticut to Virginia and Pittsburgh, Pennsylvania. Beside each bank were notations, most commonly "F-7."

F-7? F-7? He kept repeating in his mind. *What does that mean?* Then it dawned on him. *It can mean only one thing. The bank closes on Fridays at 7 P.M.*

Carr cleared his throat and, in a voice brimming with certainty, announced to the others, "I know who owns all this stuff — the Friday Night Bank Robber."

The agent was referring to the most successful bank robber in American history, a mystery man who was sticking up dozens of banks — always on a Friday evening — in the Northeast. His overall haul totaled about $2 million, which was more than the combined take of legendary outlaws Jesse James, Pretty Boy Floyd, John Dillinger, Bonnie and Clyde, and the infamous Willie Sutton, who, when asked why he robbed banks, replied, "Because that's where the money is."

THE CASE OF THE FRIDAY NIGHT BANK ROBBER

The Friday Night Bank Robber's MO was always the same: He hit rural bank branches that backed up to wooded areas. Just before closing time, the robber, who always worked alone, burst through the bank doors and, waving a handgun, shouted in a loud, menacing voice, "Don't look at me!" Even as they recoiled in horror, customers couldn't help but stare at his bizarre appearance. He wore a scary Halloween mask — sometimes that of Freddy Krueger from the Nightmare on Elm Street movies — that fit so tightly over his face and neck that no one could identify the color of his skin or hair.

Dark, bulky clothes hid his body, and gloves covered his hands. As the terror-stricken people hugged the floor, the robber pointed his weapon at them to create the impression that everyone was a potential target.

To prevent witnesses from guessing how tall he was, the thief moved quickly across the floor in a crablike crouch. He then vaulted over the counter of the teller windows in a single bound and rifled through the cash drawers, stuffing money in a black bag. Within ninety seconds, he was out the door, vanishing into the darkness without leaving a single clue.

"I've been studying this guy for eight months," Carr told the officers at the Radnor Police Department. "I know him well."

Carr, an FBI agent since 1989 who was now based in Newtown Square near Philadelphia, Pennsylvania, had plenty of experience solving difficult crimes, including bank robberies. He worked closely with the Bureau's National Center for the Analysis of Violent Crime. In September 2000, he had been asked by FBI agents in Scranton, Pennsylvania, and Albany, New York, to work up a profile and analysis of the man they believed was responsible for more than a dozen bank robberies in their districts.

Carr was an expert in profiling serial criminals — creating a list of physical, behavioral, and mental characteristics about a suspect whose identity isn't known. The typical profile is based on police-gathered evidence, witness accounts, the suspect's conduct during the crime, and psychological guesswork.

"I reviewed the case files of the bank robberies and came up with a profile of the Friday Night Bank Robber," Carr told the officers at Radnor. "He's a loner in his forties or fifties. He's a relatively mysterious person who doesn't communicate much with friends or relatives about his personal life. Few people are close to him, and I doubt if anyone knows he's a criminal.

"This guy is incredibly smart and extremely careful and spends days planning his robberies. The way he handles a gun tells me he's been in the military, and the fact that he uses different guns in his robberies tells me he's fascinated with weapons. He wants to scare people, but he won't hurt anyone unless he's forced to. So far, there've been two instances when he shot and wounded an employee and pistol-whipped another.

"His signature leap over the counter demonstrates he's in superb physical condition and a fitness fanatic. Judging from the bank surveillance videos, I guess he's anywhere from five feet four to five feet eight.

"All the robberies have occurred between October and April when it's dark and cold, so passersby are less likely to notice someone wearing gloves and bulky clothing. He strikes about ten minutes before closing, because there are fewer people in the bank, thus fewer chances someone will try to stop him."

"How do we find this guy?" an officer asked.

Waving his hand over the confiscated items, Carr replied, "Maybe one of these things will give us the clue we need."

He studied the flesh-colored Halloween masks. Some of them were hand-painted with scars and streaks to make them look more frightening. He examined the weapons — all large-caliber guns with their serial numbers filed off so they couldn't be traced. Also in the collection were books on electrical engineering and statistics as well as a tattered and yellowed *Camp Hill Handbook*.

Camp Hill was a prison near Harrisburg, Pennsylvania. The agent thumbed through the handbook and saw that the copyright indicated it was printed in 1960 when the place was a juvenile detention facility. "If my profile is correct, the robber could have spent time there as a teenager in the nineteen sixties," he told his colleagues.

The agent turned his attention to seven hand-drawn maps. They had stick drawings of landmarks such as trees, roads, parking lots, and ponds, along with arrows and dotted lines and various numbers. "I think these are maps to other bunkers," he said. "The numbers represent the paces he walks from a landmark to the site. The robber is particular and pays attention to detail, yet these maps are crude. He drew the maps this way on purpose to include only enough information to jog his memory. That way, it makes them much more difficult for anyone else to understand. I just don't know what locations these maps are referring to."

After studying one of the maps, an officer spoke up. "I think I recognize the place. It's one of the state forests near the town of Jim Thorpe, about eighty miles from here. I've ridden my mountain bike there many times."

"That's the region where many of the bank robberies occurred," Carr said.

With the help of a game warden and the crude maps, officials searched the rugged terrain for the bunkers for nearly three months without success. One day in June, however, they came across a cairn — a stacked pile of rocks — next to a turn in a deer path that was marked on the map. Penciled in the map was the word *cairn* with a number and arrow next to it. From the cairn, the searchers followed the direction of the arrow and paced off the same number of steps that was written on the map. They stopped at a three-by-three-foot rock hidden by brush and fallen limbs. When they removed the rock, they found a hand-dug bunker. Hidden inside were 44 weapons, including assault rifles, submachine guns, shotguns, and powerful handguns such as Berettas and GLOCKs. The investigators also discovered about 5,000 rounds of ammunition, holsters and magazines, and five-gallon buckets containing Halloween masks, makeup kits, disguises, fake mustaches, military gear, and rock-climbing equipment.

There was no doubt in Carr's mind that this bunker belonged to the Friday Night Bank Robber. *Why would he go to all that trouble to store these weapons?* the agent wondered. *Is he planning something bigger than a bank robbery? Is he becoming more dangerous? How many more weapons does he have? Is he turning into someone who could retaliate in a bad way if there's any kind of move made against him? He's real good at what he does and could rob banks the rest of his life, which means there's a likely chance more people could get hurt. We must find this guy and put him away for life.*

But the FBI, which had set up a 30-member task force to capture the robber, still didn't know who he was or where he was. *He's like a ghost,* the agent thought.

Eventually, other camouflaged weapons caches and bunkers were discovered. So far, the robber had been careful not to leave any fingerprints and had filed off the serial numbers on all the weapons — except for one that he had mistakenly failed to alter. A gun registration database revealed the serial number belonged to a pistol stolen in 1975 from a pawnshop in Fayetteville, North Carolina. *That's where Fort Bragg is located,* Carr thought, referring to the army base. *I wouldn't be surprised if our robber was once stationed there.*

The bunkers also contained lists of books about crime-scene techniques and statistics. *He either really likes math or he works in that field,* the agent thought. Among the items that intrigued Carr the most were videos and plaques from Dillman Karate International. A Google search showed that Dillman was a chain of more than 100 martial arts schools, known as *dojos.* Carr thought, *This could be the lead we need. The robber must have some connection with Dillman.*

Determined to track down the criminal, Carr was prepared to send agents to every Dillman dojo in the country. But first, he visited the one in Upper Darby because it was the closest dojo to the bunker.

Accompanied by a state trooper, Carr talked with the owners — a medical doctor and a high-school teacher. The agent was interested in the teacher because he fit the physical description of the robber's profile. "What do you teach?" Carr asked him. *If he says math, then he will be worth investigating.*

"I teach chemistry," the teacher replied.

The veteran agent had a knack for reading people's body language and noted that during the conversation, the teacher didn't come off as someone who was afraid to talk to authorities. *No, he's not a suspect.*

"We're looking for a man we think is into karate and might have worked out here," Carr told the owners. "He's someone between five four and five eight, medium build; in his late forties to mid-fifties, likes rock climbing, probably works as a mathematician, and tends to be a loner."

The teacher said, "That's sounds like Carl Gugasian. Nice guy, quiet, a third-degree black belt."

"What does he do for a living?" Carr asked.

"He's a self-employed statistician."

The state trooper turned to Carr and said, "That must be our man!"

"Calm down," said the agent. "Let's check him out."

At the state police substation, they ran a quick computer background check and found that the 55-year-old Carl Gugasian had a juvenile record and served time at Camp Hill Detention Center. "I feel pretty confident he's the guy we want," Carr said. After all these years, the FBI finally had attached a name to a prime suspect.

When the agent returned to his office, he asked an FBI clerk to run Gugasian's name on another database to get an address. Minutes later, he heard a scream. "What's the matter?" Carr asked her.

She replied excitedly, "Gugasian lives in an apartment complex in Radnor — right across the street from where the first bunker was found!"

Carr began learning all he could about Gugasian. Research revealed that he had served in the army and was even in Special Forces training at Fort Bragg at the time the pistol was stolen in nearby Fayetteville. A graduate of Haverford (Pennsylvania) High School, he earned a scholarship to Villanova University and graduated with a degree in electrical engineering. He later got a master's degree in systems analysis at the University of Pennsylvania and did post-graduate work in statistics and probabilities at Penn State University. *He is one smart, smart guy, and he has the training to pull off these robberies*, thought Carr, who was pleased that the profile he had created was spot-on.

The agent went to Gugasian's last known address — the Radnor Crossing Apartments. He told the manager and her assistant, "I want to ask you some questions about the guy in 119-A."

"We knew it," the manager said. "He's CIA, right?"

"No, he's not," Carr replied.

"Then he's in the witness protection program."

"No. Why do you say that?"

"Because he's weird."

"Really? How?"

"He runs fully clothed with a backpack."

"I agree. That does sound weird. Have you seen him lately?"

"No, he moved out." She checked her records and said, "He left in early April."

Right after the first bunker was discovered, the agent thought. *He obviously knows we found it.*

It didn't take the FBI long to learn that Gugasian had moved to a modest apartment seven miles away in Plymouth Meeting. A surveillance unit, which began keeping tabs on him, saw that he worked out a lot, went to the library, and did all the typical things that any ordinary citizen would do. A bachelor who dated but never married, Gugasian was a health-food fanatic and a devotee of yoga and meditation. He owned an older model van worth $2,000, an old car worth $1,000, and a dirt bike. He had two bank accounts totaling $500,000.

So far, the FBI didn't have any direct evidence — other than circumstantial — that linked him to any crime. He hadn't attempted a bank robbery since the first bunker had been discovered. By now, the agents had found 20 bunkers, including one that yielded 54 fingerprints of his. Carr felt confident that Gugasian would stick to his MO, which meant he wouldn't try to hit another bank until late fall or winter.

He'll lie low because he's not really sure what we know and when we'll come knocking on his door, Carr thought. *I'm sure he was waiting for us to find him in April, but when we didn't, he probably became more comfortable. He might be thinking,* Well, maybe I've done a good job concealing my identity because they don't know who I am. *Oh, yes we do, Carl.*

The FBI was gathering evidence against Gugasian when its priorities drastically changed following the 9/11 terrorist attacks. Agents and surveillance teams that had been on the Gugasian task force were now working on terrorism-related investigations.

However, by the end of the year, the FBI had obtained an indictment against Gugasian. Carr had an arrest warrant for him, but before collaring him, the agent wanted to secure some new search warrants.

On Monday, January 28, 2002, Carr learned that a rural bank branch, located next to a wooded area in Yardley, Pennsylvania, had been robbed the previous Friday evening by a masked gunman shortly before closing. *He's back at it again*, thought the agent.

Because the agent was dealing with other top-priority cases at the time, it took him a week to assemble a team for the arrest. To his concern, another bank was robbed outside of Harrisburg the following Friday night.

We can't wait any longer, Carr thought. *We have to make our move against him. He's getting too comfortable. If we don't nab him now, I'm afraid this guy is going to hurt someone.*

THE CASE OF THE FRIDAY NIGHT BANK ROBBER

Two SWAT teams — nicknamed "Blue" and "White" — were given the task of arresting Gugasian in the safest way possible. The Blue team was a surveillance unit that followed him as he ran errands, while the White team stood by outside his apartment. Carr wanted to avoid arresting him at his apartment out of concern that Gugasian would barricade himself and use weapons against the agents. Carr, who was with the White team, stayed in constant radio contact with the Blue team as it tailed the suspect for an hour.

When Gugasian stopped at a bank, an alarmed agent radioed Carr, "He's going into a bank!"

"Relax," Carr replied. "He doesn't go into banks during the day to rob them. He's conducting business. Unless he's all covered up in dark clothes, don't stop him."

After leaving the bank, the suspect drove downtown and parked his car by the Philadelphia Free Library. That's when the Blue team pulled up in an unmarked van, jumped out, and arrested him.

"We got him!" an agent radioed to Carr. "We arrested him without incident and caught him completely by surprise. He was unarmed."

A search of Gugasian's apartment turned up two loaded weapons. As Carr expected, the suspect's apartment was extremely neat. Even the socks in his drawers were rolled up. But to Carr's surprise, the kitchen was a mess with dirty dishes and pots in the sink and on the counter.

THE CASE OF THE FRIDAY NIGHT BANK ROBBER

Shortly after the arrest, Carr went down to the processing room to talk with Gugasian. But the robber wasn't cooperative and ended their brief conversation by asking for a lawyer.

Over the next eight months, the FBI prepared for trial because Gugasian had pleaded not guilty to bank robbery charges. He refused to admit anything. But shortly before the trial was set to begin, his attorney went to Carr and said, "He wants to talk to you. You get one shot. And depending on how that goes, he'll decide if he wants to cooperate." Gugasian was facing life in prison if convicted on all counts. Cooperation could possibly get him a lighter sentence.

When Carr visited the defendant, the agent didn't act judgmental, and he treated him with the respect he would give any person, so Gugasian opened up to him. At first all the FBI knew was that he had been robbing banks for 13 years, beginning in 1988. But he confessed to the agent that his first bank robbery was in 1972 and that he had robbed between 50 and 60 banks — twice what the FBI thought. He displayed an uncanny memory for detail, remembering places and dates.

"Thirty years is a long time to carry around a secret, Carl," the agent said. Although he was stunned to hear that Gugasian had been hitting banks for three decades, Carr kept a poker face because he wanted the robber to believe the FBI knew everything.

The agent gained his trust. At Carr's urging, Gugasian directed agents to the seven cleverly camouflaged bunkers that they hadn't found. He also confessed to dozens of bank robberies.

Carr became his confidante and learned more about how this bright man ended up on the wrong side of the law: Gugasian said he came from a dysfunctional family in Haverford Township, Pennsylvania, where his Armenian-born father ran an auto repair shop and ruled the house with an iron fist over the boy's meek mother and two younger brothers. When he was 14 years old, Gugasian and three boys were arrested after they broke into a school, stole musical instruments, and pawned them. Claiming the teen was a loser who would never amount to anything, his father refused to bail him out, so he spent the whole summer in a juvenile detention facility. When he got out, he worked alone as a burglar until the night he broke into a Philadelphia candy store and was shot in the rear end by a policeman. Gugasian did 18 months at Camp Hill for that crime.

Upon his release in 1964, he returned to high school as a junior. The guidance counselor told him, "You've got this bad arrest record. This is going to follow you the rest of your life, and you're going to have a difficult time getting into college and getting a job. It will be twice as hard for you, so you need to work twice as hard."

By staying out of trouble and applying himself, Gugasian earned his college degree and then enlisted in the army during the height of the Vietnam War. Training to be a Special Forces soldier, he put in for an assignment that required top secret clearance, but he wasn't chosen. He assumed it was because of his juvenile history. (Carr would later discover that Gugasian's past had nothing to do with it. The person selected over him was simply better qualified.)

After serving in the military, he returned to college life for post-graduate work. Despite his impressive academic credentials, he was convinced no one would ever hire him because of his haunted past.

After reading a newspaper article about a man who had robbed a bank of $80,000, Gugasian decided to make his living robbing banks. To his relatives and acquaintances, who knew nothing of his criminal ways, he was a quiet self-employed statistician and professional gambler who earned $7,000 a month. He dutifully paid his income tax and his required contributions to Social Security and Medicare out of his ill-gotten gains.

Gugasian told Carr that he would spend two or three days at a time in the woods outside each targeted bank, carefully monitoring the routines of the employees and their customers. On the day of the robbery, he would drive his van to within ten miles of the bank. Then he would take out his off-road dirt bike and ride it into the woods until he was three miles from the bank, and walk the rest of the way. After the robbery, Gugasian, who was doused in scent-deflecting fragrances to confuse police dogs, would flee into the woods and stash the money and clothes in a hiding place. Then he would ride his bike to the van, load it, and drive off. A few days later, he would return to the woods and retrieve the clothes and stolen money.

"I look at it as a victimless crime," he told Carr. "I didn't see anything wrong with what I was doing because I was taking money from banks, not from people. It wasn't like I was hurting anybody."

"But you were hurting people, Carl. You shot a bank manager in Jim Thorpe."

"That was an accident."

"You shot a woman bank employee in Kingston, New York."

"Another accident."

"And you smacked a guy with your gun in Wilkes-Barre, Pennsylvania."

"I had to. He was trying to be a hero."

"Carl, in order to get that money, you had to go through people, who were traumatized. Some of those people will never be the same. Even though you got money from banks, you were hurting people all along."

Gugasian paused and stared at the floor. When he looked up at Carr, he murmured, "I never thought of it that way before."

"You know, Carl, you're a smart guy. Over the last thirty years, you made a couple million dollars. But the truth is you probably could have made more money working legitimately.

And you wouldn't have had to worry about all the stress associated with robbing banks."

"I couldn't get an honest job because of my juvenile record. I had to rob banks."

"No, you didn't, Carl. Everybody has a choice. And you chose the wrong one."

Gugasian faced a possible 115 years in prison. As part of a plea bargain, he agreed to fully cooperate with the FBI and pleaded guilty to five bank robberies. (Too much time had elapsed to prosecute most of the other cases.) In December 2003, U.S. District Court Judge Anita Brody sentenced him to 17½ years in federal prison without parole, fined him $12,000, and ordered him to repay the five banks $201,215 — the amount he stole from them.

A week after he was sentenced, Gugasian was interviewed on videotape for a training film about bank robbery investigations that the FBI distributed nationally to police academies and law-enforcement training programs.

Carr and Gugasian still have a good relationship and talk about once a year. Gugasian has been a model prisoner, teaching advanced math to fellow felons. "Maybe getting caught was the best thing that ever happened to him," Carr says. "Today, he has an opportunity to give something back and help people, to reach out and have real friendships and a real human life."

Gugasian will be released when he's 73 years old.

THE CASE OF THE GEORGIA JIHADISTS

Ever since Special Agent Mark Richards was assigned to the international terrorism squad after the 9/11 attacks, he had investigated countless suspicious activities that turned out harmless. But the evidence he was gathering about two young men in the Atlanta area told him this case could be serious — deadly serious.

It was up to him and his fellow agents to unravel a frightening conspiracy of terror with ties to Muslim extremists in other parts of the world.

In summer 2005, the FBI received a tip from the Canadian Security Intelligence Service (CSIS) — Canada's spy agency — of suspicious behavior of Ehsanul "Shifa" Sadequee, 18, of Roswell, Georgia, and Syed Haris Ahmed, 21, of Dawsonville, Georgia. The two had spent six days in Toronto in March visiting three people who were under investigation by international antiterrorism authorities.

The CSIS turned over copies of emails the two Atlanta-area men had exchanged with the Canadian suspects about planning terrorist attacks in the United States and getting military training at a camp run by a group allied with al-Qaeda.

We need to figure out what these two guys are up to, Richards thought. *If they are terrorists, we need to capture them and dismantle their terrorist cell before they carry out their violent plots.*

In August 2005, the Joint Terrorism Task Force (JTTF), headed by the FBI's Atlanta division, opened an investigation. Richards was the case agent for Ahmed, and Special Agent Michael Scherck was the case agent for Sadequee. A background check revealed that neither suspect had a criminal record. Sadequee was an American-born citizen whose parents were from the South Asian country of Bangladesh. After spending part of his childhood in Atlanta, he attended high school in Canada, where he also studied the Koran. He spent time in Bangladesh before moving to Roswell, Georgia, where he lived with his sister and worked part time at a women's rights organization.

Syed Haris Ahmed was a naturalized American citizen who was born in Pakistan and moved to the United States when he was 12 years old. He possessed both a Pakistani and a U.S. passport. His family was highly educated; his father was a college professor. Although Ahmed sometimes lived with his parents and siblings in Dawsonville, his primary residence was a rented ramshackle house in downtown Atlanta where he attended the Georgia Institute of Technology on a scholarship. He also held a part-time job at a Muslim perfumery in an Atlanta suburb.

Nothing indicated that these two were potential jihadists other than the emails that Canadian authorities had given to the FBI. But Richards knew that terrorist organizations try to recruit jihadists who have clean criminal backgrounds. This case received the highest priority. *What do these emails mean?* the agent wondered. *What will they be doing in the future — in the next few days, weeks, months? Where are they now?*

The FBI immediately put Sadequee under surveillance, but couldn't for Ahmed because he had left the previous month for Pakistan, where he supposedly was attending an Islamic school.

The investigation revealed that the two were friends and members of a group of Muslim students from Georgia Tech and Georgia State University. "Most of the young Muslims just want to hang out together on campus," an informant told the FBI. "But Ahmed and Sadequee are the most radical of the group and like to wear traditional Muslim outfits. The others nicknamed them the 'Taliban Brothers.'"

On August 18, 2005, Sadequee flew from Atlanta to New York for a connecting flight to Bangladesh. Because he was under surveillance, the FBI knew his plans, so two JTTF agents were waiting for him when he arrived at JFK Airport in New York. They asked him questions about his travel plans in Bangladesh, his prior foreign travel, and his associates and contacts.

During the interview, Sadequee said he was going to Bangladesh to get married and would return to the U.S. with his bride once she obtained a visa, which could take up to nine months. When asked about his previous foreign travel, Sadequee replied that he had gone to Canada alone on a Greyhound bus the previous January and stayed with his aunt in Toronto. However, when the agents asked for her name, Sadequee said he knew her only as "Manju Auntie" and couldn't recall the name of her husband. At the end of the interview, the agents politely wished him well, and he caught his flight to Bangladesh.

While he was being questioned, other federal agents conducted a routine search of his checked luggage without his knowledge. They found a CD concealed in the lining of his suitcase. It contained encrypted files that FBI technical experts were unable to decode. The agents also found a hidden Fairfax County Visitors' Center map of the Washington, D.C., and Alexandria, Virginia, areas as well as a scrap of paper with a Pakistani phone number. The FBI later discovered that the number belonged to the cell phone of Aabid Hussein Khan, a senior member of a terrorist organization aligned with al-Qaeda.

THE CASE OF THE GEORGIA JIHADISTS

The following day, Ahmed returned from a month's trip to Pakistan, landing at Hartsfield-Jackson Atlanta International Airport, where federal agents were waiting to question him. During the interview, Ahmed said he traveled to Pakistan to visit family and to seek Islamic schooling. He added that he stayed with relatives while he was there.

When asked about other foreign travel, Ahmed said he went to Toronto in March with his friend Sadequee to visit friends and family. Ahmed added that he and Sadequee stayed with a friend, and not with Sadequee's aunt.

Richards found it suspicious that Sadequee left for Bangladesh the day before Ahmed returned home. Also strange was that Ahmed's account of the trip to Canada differed from Sadequee's.

The FBI obtained records from Greyhound showing that two tickets were issued to Sadequee and Ahmed for travel from Atlanta to Toronto on March 6 with a return date of March 13. Bank records revealed that Sadequee used his debit card to pay $280 for the tickets on February 26. Immigration and Customs Enforcement records showed that Sadequee and Ahmed crossed the border from Canada back into the United States moments apart on March 12.

That proved that Sadequee had lied about when he had traveled to Canada — and lying to a federal agent is against the law. Richards was convinced that Sadequee also lied to agents when he said he stayed with his aunt in Toronto, and that Ahmed lied about the reason for their trip.

THE CASE OF THE GEORGIA JIHADISTS

The case now received top priority. *If they're planning something violent, we need to prevent it,* Richards thought. *I don't want to be investigating another 9/11 or a mass murder.* As one of the lead investigators, Richards knew that for him and his colleagues, it meant working nights, weekends, and holidays.

Using new antiterrorism laws, the FBI secretly monitored Ahmed's emails in Atlanta, where he resumed his studies at Georgia Tech. The emails revealed the real reason for his visit to Pakistan: He had planned to attend a terrorist training camp but had backed out at the last minute. He wrote that he regretted his lack of resolve and vowed to make another attempt at getting terrorist training.

In late August, the FBI obtained the suspects' cell phone records. They revealed that both men were billed for roaming charges while in Washington on April 10–11. A check of their credit-card accounts failed to show any activity during their trip, which to Richards meant that they paid cash for their meals, gas, and other expenses. *What were they doing there?* Richards wondered. *Were they casing possible targets for terrorist acts?*

The answer came by way of Europe. In October, police in Bosnia thwarted a terrorist attack by arresting two young men who were armed and wearing suicide vests. The pair had left behind martyrdom videos — personal videos they had made as their last statements before launching their planned suicide attack. The police also found telephone numbers, including one belonging to Younis Tsouli, who called himself "Irhabi 007" (Arabic for "Terrorist 007"). Tsouli, who lived in London, was a notorious recruiter for al-Qaeda in Iraq. As a "cyber-jihadist," he sent violent videos and terrorist how-to videos and manuals to Muslim youth around the world via the Internet.

Police in London then raided Tsouli's home, where they seized his computer. While analyzing the hard drive, British investigators found something of great interest to Richards and his team — video of landmarks in Washington taken by none other than Ahmed and Sadequee.

The 62 clips that the two shot while in Ahmed's pickup truck were mostly of symbolic targets for potential terrorist attacks, including the United States Capitol, the World Bank headquarters, the Masonic Temple, and a complex of large fuel-storage tanks near I-95 in northern Virginia. The video clips revealed just how close someone could get to these places because they focused on security stations, guards, entrances, fences, and barriers. On one of the clips, the two were driving past the Pentagon when Sadequee said, with obvious pride in his voice, "This is where our brothers attacked."

When Richards saw the video, he became alarmed. *Now we know why they were in Washington. They were doing more than just casing the area for potential targets. They were also trying to establish their credentials with terrorists.* He noted that all the targets were on the map that Sadequee had hidden in his suitcase.

Further investigation revealed that Ahmed had put the video clips on a thumb drive and given it to another person in Pakistan, who emailed it to Tsouli. Evidence also surfaced that Sadequee had emailed the video clips to various websites that promoted violent jihad. The emails were labeled "Jimmy's 13th birthday" and "Volleyball practice."

The FBI continued to monitor all of Ahmed's communications as well as keep the slender, bearded young man under constant surveillance. He was still attending classes, seeing friends, going to mosque, and not doing anything outwardly that seemed suspicious — except for one thing.

Whenever he drove his car, he acted paranoid. He would make quick U-turns, speed up and slow down, and turn at the last possible second — maneuvers designed to evade a possible surveillance team. But he never could tell which, if any, vehicle was tailing him. He didn't know that sometimes it wasn't even a car; it was a helicopter.

One fall day, an FBI agent who had been tailing Ahmed saw him sit down at a computer at the Georgia Tech library and pull up a website showing how to make explosives.

When Richards heard about it, he thought, *We don't know what Ahmed is doing. Is he going to Georgia Tech to get an engineering degree so he can learn about making weapons of mass destruction? Will he carry out a terrorist mission? And what is Sadequee really doing in Bangladesh?*

THE CASE OF THE GEORGIA JIHADISTS

From antiterrorism agencies overseas, Richards learned that shortly after Sadequee arrived in Bangladesh, he was helping Tsouli set up a new violent jihadist organization called "Al-Qaeda in Northern Europe," which was going to be based in Sweden. Sadequee even sought a visa that would allow him to relocate there. But then Tsouli was arrested in London. Around the same time, another leader of the proposed new group, Mirsad Bektašević, was arrested in the Eastern European city of Sarajevo. Known by his nickname "Maximus," Bektašević was in possession of more than 20 pounds of plastic explosives, a suicide belt with a detonator, and a firearm with a silencer. Authorities also found a video recorded by the terrorist showing an arsenal of semiautomatic weapons, grenades, explosives, and other arms. In addition, the video demonstrated how to make detonators and how to place a grenade booby trap in a forest.

Of heightened interest to the FBI's investigation of Ahmed and Sadequee, evidence was found in Sarajevo that revealed Sadequee had been in touch with Bektašević by phone and email as recently as three days before Bektašević's arrest. The two had been discussing the silencer and explosives Bektašević had acquired for the group.

Back in the United States, Ahmed was making contact with other terrorism suspects under FBI investigation. One of them, a Georgia Tech student who was a friend of Sadequee's, was so worried he would be arrested that he agreed to cooperate with the FBI. He told agents that earlier in the year, he, Sadequee, and Ahmed spent many hours in online chat rooms dedicated to militant Islamic radicals. They watched training videos by Osama bin Laden and the Taliban, and practiced jihad attack techniques with paintball guns in north Georgia. He said he broke away from the other two when they started talking about attacking the White House and visiting terrorist groups in Canada and the Middle East.

Meanwhile, Ahmed tried to thwart the government from secretly monitoring his emails. He relied on multiple email addresses and encrypted materials. He also used coded words in Urdu, the language spoken in Pakistan. But he was no match for the Bureau. The FBI knew he was keeping in touch with Sadequee and supporters of terrorism in the United States, Canada, the United Kingdom, Pakistan, and other countries.

Ahmed and another jihadist supporter in Chicago devised a numbering system to refer to stages of their faith in jihad from one to three, with three being ready to do battle. An email to Ahmed in November said that they were almost at stage three. In other monitored emails with terrorists such as Aabid Hussein Khan, Ahmed discussed financing a trip to Pakistan for paramilitary training and then joining the *mujahedeen* (holy warriors) in violent jihad. Ahmed also emailed Sadequee about going to a mountain region in Afghanistan for terrorism training.

THE CASE OF THE GEORGIA JIHADISTS

In January 2006, agents who were tailing Ahmed saw him go into the Home Depot and buy a piece of PVC pipe that was four feet long and six inches in diameter. Richards knew Ahmed had researched bomb-making techniques online and had shaved his head, as some jihadists have done before an attack. Concerned that Ahmed planned to make an improvised explosive device, the agent conferred with the FBI's bomb techs. They assured him that the pipe was not the right dimension for an effective bomb. Still, Richards felt it was time to question Ahmed about the purchase.

The agent sent a police detective, who was a member of the JTTF, to the perfumery where Ahmed worked part time. "Mr. Ahmed," said the detective, "this is kind of ridiculous and I'm embarrassed to bring this up, but someone saw you buy a PVC pipe at the Home Depot and got your license plate because of the fear it could be used for a bomb. We have to follow up on every terrorism lead and every suspicious activity. It's no big deal, just routine. Why did you buy it?"

"I'm an engineering student at Georgia Tech," Ahmed replied. "It's for a class project."

The detective wanted to get a feel for what Ahmed would say and how he would react. Throughout the brief interview, the suspect remained relatively calm and answered all the questions politely. At no time did he appear irritated or nervous.

As the weeks went by, Richards wondered why Ahmed and Sadequee weren't in touch more often if they were involved in a conspiracy. *Maybe they are communicating in other ways that we haven't uncovered,* the agent thought. Little was known about Sadequee's activities in Bangladesh other than he had made plenty of contacts with members of terrorist organizations.

Worried that Sadequee could be plotting an attack from overseas, Richards decided to confront Ahmed with the help of a JTTF member — DeKalb County Police Detective Khalid Sediqi, a Muslim who hoped to gain the suspect's trust. At the time, Richards had no plans to arrest Ahmed; the goal was to get him to talk, especially about Sadequee's plans.

The two agents approached the suspect as he was walking home from class. Richards told him they were following up on the report about the PVC pipe. Although Ahmed had every right to refuse to cooperate, he invited them into his house.

The conversation remained friendly in tone, but Richards detected a slight change in Ahmed's manner when the agent asked him where he had been traveling during the previous 18 months. Ahmed replied that he had been in Pakistan to attend the wedding of his cousin. He failed to mention his trips to Canada and Washington, D.C.

"When did you go to D.C.?" Richards asked.

The question stunned Ahmed, and at first, he nervously denied being there.

"Well, we've got your cell phone records that show you were in Washington, D.C., in April of last year," the agent told him. "What were you doing there?"

Ahmed didn't want to answer. "My heart is beating really fast right now," he said.

Richards kept pressing him, but Ahmed didn't want to give up any more information. By now, though, Sediqi had used his Muslim connection with Ahmed to build some rapport with him. "Hey, my brother, you and I are Muslims," the detective reminded the suspect. "Agent Richards and I are just trying to get to the bottom of this and understand what the truth is. And the truth is what we're all about as Muslims, right?"

Over the next week, Richards and Sediqi questioned Ahmed four more times — and each time, elements of his story changed and the truth slowly came out. Ahmed, who was unaware that he was being secretly recorded, signed statements about his answers.

When confronted with evidence of the Canada trip, he admitted that he and Sadequee went to Toronto to meet with like-minded Islamic extremists. During their week-long stay, the two met regularly with at least three people who were subjects of an FBI international terrorism investigation.

He said that they discussed strategic locations in the United States suitable for a terrorist strike, including oil refineries and military bases. They also plotted how to disable the Global Positioning System in an effort to disrupt military and commercial communications and traffic. The group developed a plan for going to Pakistan, where they hoped to receive military training at a terrorist-sponsored camp. But Ahmed tried to downplay the meetings, telling Richards and Sediqi, "Look, man, it was nothing. It was just childish talk and stuff like that."

Under more intense questioning, he confessed that he had gone to Pakistan the previous July hoping to be recruited into a jihadi training camp "where I could learn how to fight Muslim oppressors everywhere."

As the interviews became more grueling for Ahmed, he became increasingly defensive and weary. Still trying to minimize his role, he asked Richards and Sediqi, "Wouldn't it be safer for America if I just leave the country?"

"No," Sediqi replied. "I think it's going to be safer if you sit here and tell me what's going on."

"Nothing is going on, man," Ahmed countered.

They warned him that it was in his best interest to tell them the truth. Sediqi told Ahmed that if he tried to conceal Sadequee's activities, he was just as guilty as his friend — and the consequences would be severe. "I'm saying no more Georgia Tech," Sediqi said. "I'm saying no more *masjid* [mosque]. I'm talking about praying in a six-by-six cell." The agents tried to get his full cooperation, but Ahmed kept dodging their questions, giving up only bits and pieces of information reluctantly.

During the third interview, Ahmed finally confessed that the Washington video clips were his idea. He had used his father's camera to shoot the various landmarks. He said Sadequee put the clips they made online so they could be accessed by "the brothers," meaning Muslim extremists.

Ahmed admitted the videos would be helpful to "plan something."

"Plan what?" Richards asked.

"Some kind of terrorist act," Ahmed mumbled. "I don't know."

Trying to downplay his and Sadequee's actions, he added, "There is nothing to be worried about. We are just stupid, childish. You know we did, yeah, a stupid mistake. We went and took a video, but in reality, it means nothing. You look at the video. The quality is so stupid, you know. It had nothing of value whatsoever."

Sediqi fired back, "You think it's silly. You think it's stupid. But people are getting arrested and going to jail for it."

At one point, Ahmed said that it was harmless excitement that led him to shoot the video. "We could be spies for the people over there," said Ahmed, referring to extremists overseas. "It's like, uh, thrilling to be undercover and stuff like that."

While trying to mislead the agents, Ahmed made increasingly incriminating statements. In his next interview two days later, he revealed that because of his jihadist beliefs, he wanted to pull off a terrorist attack against Dobbins Air Reserve Base in Marietta, Georgia, where he once lived. He also considered an attack on oil refineries in Texas to raise the price of oil and bring more money back to the Middle East because the region's oil "is Muslim property, and it's being stolen," he told the agents.

After the series of interviews, Richards told Ahmed not to talk with Sadequee. However, two days later, Ahmed, who was unaware he was under 24-hour surveillance, visited Sadequee's brother in Roswell.

With agents secretly listening, Ahmed told him, "I don't know what to do. They're [the FBI] trying to figure out what we're doing." He said he feared his house was bugged and that he needed to warn Sadequee. The brother then took him to a service station down the street where Ahmed made a call on a pay phone to Sadequee.

Two days later, agents followed Ahmed to a public library where he used one of its computers to email Sadequee. From a secret French Yahoo! account, Ahmed told his friend "the dogs" (his nasty reference to the agents) had grilled him and knew all about the trips to Toronto and Washington, D.C. He urged Sadequee not to return to the United States.

It's clear Ahmed won't cooperate with us, Richards thought. *It's time to bring him in.* After the FBI presented its case against Ahmed to the grand jury, he was indicted and then arrested without incident on March 23 on federal charges of conspiring to provide material support to terrorist organizations.

The following month, authorities in Dhaka, Bangladesh, tracked down Sadequee and apprehended him. Under an arrangement with the United States government, they turned him over to American agents, who then flew Sadequee back to Atlanta on a government plane. Sadequee, who refused to talk to agents on the flight home, was charged with conspiring to provide material support to terrorists.

With both men locked up and awaiting trial, Richards could finally relax — along with the nearly 150 people who ultimately worked on the case, including members of the JTTF; FBI agents, analysts, and technicians; detectives and officers from Atlanta-area law enforcement departments; federal attorneys; Border Patrol and Customs agents; and other authorities.

There was still much more work to do to prepare for trial, but at least Richards felt proud of the FBI's effort in this phase of the investigation. *We took two potential terrorists off the street,* he told himself. *I don't know how far they would have gone. Only those two can answer that. All I know is that if they were planning to do something big, they aren't going to do it now.*

In June 2009, Ahmed was convicted of conspiracy to provide material support to terrorist organizations. Two months later,

Sadequee was found guilty of four counts of supporting terrorists and a foreign terrorist organization. In December, Ahmed and Sadequee were sentenced to 13 years and 17 years, respectively, followed by 30 years of supervised release for both.

The two were the only Americans linked to a terror network that spread from the United States and Canada to the United Kingdom, Pakistan, Bangladesh, and Bosnia and Herzegovina, and led to the arrest of 42 suspects. Among those arrested were Ahmed's and Sadequee's three like-minded Canadian jihadist friends who were nabbed with 15 others in a series of high-profile antiterrorism raids in June 2006. Known as the "Toronto 18," the Canadian extremists were charged with participating in a terrorist group, importing weapons, and planning a bombing.

Two of the most notorious international terrorist figures that Ahmed and Sadequee had communicated with were nabbed in the United Kingdom. Younis Tsouli was convicted in 2007 of incitement to commit acts of terrorism and was sentenced to 17 years in prison. A year later, Aabid Hussein Khan was convicted on terrorism charges and sentenced to 12 years. Another captured international terrorist who had been in contact with Sadequee was Mirsad Bektašević. He was convicted in 2007 of plotting a terrorist attack and was sentenced to eight years in prison.

"Protecting the United States from terrorist attacks is the highest priority of every FBI employee," said FBI Atlanta

THE CASE OF THE GEORGIA JIHADISTS

Special Agent in Charge Gregory Jones. "Working with our law enforcement and intelligence community partners, the FBI was fortunate enough to have disrupted and dismantled a group whose stated goal was to provide support to those engaged in terrorism."

THE CASE OF THE ARAGAO ABDUCTIONS

Wealthy Brazilian-born businessman Alceu Aragao paced the living room of his swank penthouse suite in a luxury high-rise condominium overlooking the ocean off Miami Beach, Florida. It was Tuesday morning, December 14, 1999. His wife, Christine, 34; nine-year-old son, Alceu Jr.; and one-year-old baby, Alex, had been missing since the previous night.

Special Agents Jim Lewis and Ed Knapp, and Renae McDermott, of the Miami Violent Crime Unit, had been called in by the local police to assist in the case. The agents were now listening intently as the worried husband and father described what happened.

"We were all at a Christmas party last night across the street — my wife, Junior, Alex, and our daughter, Juliana,"

Alceu told them. "About nine P.M., Alex was getting cranky, so Christine said she wanted to take him and Junior and walk home and put them to bed. I didn't want them to cross the busy street in the dark, so I insisted that Christine take them home in my Porsche."

Alceu said that when he and Juliana, 12, arrived home a half hour later, Christine and the two boys weren't there. Thinking she went to the store for milk, he called Christine's cell phone but she didn't pick up. He called again and again. Growing frantic by the hour, Alceu went down to the underground parking garage and hopped into his Ferrari, one of his five cars, to look for them. On his way out, he noticed that his Porsche was parked but the family's black Lincoln Navigator SUV was gone. He drove up and down Collins Avenue, one of Miami Beach's busiest streets, looking for the Navigator. At about 2 A.M., he stopped a police officer and asked for help in finding his missing wife and children.

Agent Lewis was aware that cases like this often turn out to be nothing more than a domestic dispute: The wife takes off with the kids after a heated argument with the husband. But Lewis knew better than to jump to any quick conclusions. His years of experience told him to follow the evidence to see where it would lead.

While listening to Alceu, the agent paid attention to the man's mannerisms and behavior, looking for any signs that might indicate he was lying. Although Alceu was extremely worried about his loved ones, he answered all questions in a calm, open, cooperative manner. *One of the top things on the to-do list is to get him to take a polygraph test so hopefully we can eliminate him as a suspect,* Lewis thought.

The agent and his colleagues went down to the parking garage and inspected the area around the family's cars. They noticed tiny drops of blood on the floor by the Porsche. They also found what appeared to be heel marks and fingernail scrapes on the cement floor as if someone had been dragged away from the vehicle.

"It's weird that the victims could have been abducted from their own building, because this is a secure parking garage with valet parkers and a security officer," Lewis told his partners. Their minds were spinning with questions: *Were Christine and the kids really kidnapped? Is someone in the family involved? Is Alceu himself behind this? Is someone who wants his money holding them for ransom?* "Right now everyone is a suspect," Lewis reminded the others.

The agent questioned the 44-year-old businessman and learned that he and his wife were native Brazilians who met in Miami and married there. Alceu was a former race-car driver who became incredibly wealthy by starting several businesses, including an electronics import/export firm.

Believing there was a strong possibility that a kidnapping had occurred, Lewis formed a task force of agents and area police and set up a temporary command post in the Aragaos' penthouse. Devices were ready to record any ransom calls that might come in on Alceu's landline or cell phone. An expert in negotiations arrived to help with any communication with the kidnapper or kidnappers. After a BOLO (be-on-the-lookout) for the family's SUV was issued to area police departments, a helicopter cruised up and down Miami Beach in search of the missing vehicle.

No one knew where Christine and her boys were or whether they were hurt. Worst of all, no one knew what fate awaited the victims.

Investigators checked the condo's surveillance cameras for clues. The footage showed the Porsche entering the garage shortly after 9 P.M. and the window-tinted Navigator leaving a few minutes later. But there were no cameras that indicated what had happened to the missing Aragaos.

Members of the task force interviewed everyone in the building — residents, security guards, and parking valets — asking if they had seen or heard anything suspicious. None had except for one resident, a woman on the first floor. She said sometime after 9 P.M., she heard a woman's screams coming from the parking garage. The resident immediately reported it to the security guard, who sent a parking valet to check it out. The valet reported back that everything was fine.

The keys to the Navigator were kept upstairs in an office. *Whoever did this had to have access to the office and know where to look for the keys,* Lewis thought.

Agent Knapp interviewed the parking valets and security guards. One of the valets drew his interest the most —

Venezuelan immigrant Jean Carlo Ferreira, 22, who had been working at the condominium for about a year and also had a part-time job as a parking valet at a local restaurant. He was extremely friendly toward the Aragaos, especially Junior, and, as a trusted employee, had access to all their vehicles.

"There's something wrong about that guy," Knapp told Lewis. "He changed his work shift to be on duty last night. When I interviewed him, he seemed like he had the weight of the world on his shoulders. He was the one who checked out the scream and reported back that everything was fine. I think he knows more than he's letting on."

"Let's polygraph him," Lewis said. "In fact, let's polygraph all the employees so Ferreira won't feel like he's a suspect."

Before the workers were tested, Alceu submitted to a polygraph. The results showed he answered questions without any signs of deception, so he was cleared. All but one of the employees who were given the test also passed. The only person who failed was Ferreira, who repeatedly denied any involvement. Convinced that he played a role in the Aragaos' disappearance, the agents considered him a prime suspect. But they didn't have enough evidence to hold him. Knapp, who was assigned the responsibility to investigate him, put Ferreira under 24-hour surveillance to see who he talked to and where he went. Agents were hoping Ferreira would lead them to the victims.

THE CASE OF THE ARAGAO ABDUCTIONS

The agents waited and wondered when Alceu would receive a call demanding a ransom from the kidnappers. "Try to keep them on the line as long as possible so our tech agents can trace the incoming call and get its location," Lewis told him.

The first call came on Tuesday, about 18 hours after the abduction. It was from Christine. She didn't say much — just that she and the kids were alive and that Alceu should check Juliana's email for a message from the kidnappers. The call lasted less than 30 seconds — too short a time for technicians to get a fix on the call's location. When Alceu checked Juliana's computer, there was no email from the kidnappers.

At least Christine and the boys are safe . . . for now, Lewis thought.

Alceu spent a majority of the time at the FBI's field office in Miami. Agents were shadowing him, ready to record each call that came in on his cell phone. A person who could translate Portuguese — the Aragaos' native language — was also by his side so agents could understand what was being said in real time.

Christine made several more brief calls, some in Portuguese and some that made little sense. She said that when she and the kids were abducted, they rode in the Navigator for about 15 to 20 minutes and were now being kept in a run-down house. She talked repeatedly about being with people who wanted to save her and the children from the Brazilian Mafia.

THE CASE OF THE ARAGAO ABDUCTIONS

"Her voice sounds robotic," Alceu told Lewis after one call. "She talks in a way that leads me to believe she's being told what to say. She sounds confused."

Meanwhile, Knapp and another agent tailed Ferreira to his other job as a valet parker at a restaurant in nearby Coconut Grove. On Wednesday night at 10:30 P.M., they watched him leave the place during a torrential rainstorm to make a ten-minute call from an outdoor pay phone.

"It must have been an emotional call judging by the way Ferreira was gesturing wildly throughout the conversation," Knapp told Lewis. "It had to be important because he was out there getting soaking wet. There's a good chance he was talking to someone involved in the abduction."

Through a subpoena, the FBI learned the number that Ferreira called belonged to Ewin Martinez, who lived in the Miami suburb of Kendall. A background check of Martinez, 46, showed he was a Venezuelan immigrant with a minor criminal record. The FBI also managed to obtain Ferreira's cell phone records, which revealed he had made a flurry of calls to Martinez in the hours before and after the kidnapping.

By now, nearly 100 law-enforcement officials were working on the case. "We aren't going to stop until we have a successful resolution and bring that family home safely," Lewis told the task force. This was his first major case as lead investigator, and the pressure was building. He reminded himself he had joined the FBI because he wanted to work on tough cases just like this one. With the full resources of the FBI behind him, he felt confident of success. "We're going to catch these guys," he vowed to his colleagues.

Christine made several more calls to Alceu. She tried to convince him to bring Juliana and meet with the kidnappers. She said they had been ordered to kill the entire family for the Brazilian Mafia, but they couldn't bring themselves to carry it out. To trick the Mafia, they needed to fake a photo showing the entire family was dead, and that's why Alceu and Juliana needed to meet them.

Lewis was convinced it was a dangerous ruse to lure Alceu. There was no way the agents were going to put him and Juliana in harm's way.

During an afternoon call on Friday, Alceu managed to keep Christine on the line longer than usual. It was just enough time for the technicians to finally pinpoint her location to a specific address. An FBI SWAT emergency assault team joined other agents in unmarked vehicles and rushed to the area. Staying out of sight down the street, the SWAT team was ready to strike if necessary, while other agents kept the house under constant surveillance.

Lewis discovered that the residence — a small, bland, cement-block three-bedroom, two-bath house — was owned by a couple who didn't live there but rented it out on a short-term basis. The person who was currently renting it for three weeks was Ewin Martinez. Authorities quickly determined the owners had nothing to do with the abduction.

Plans were drafted to rescue the Aragaos and nab the kidnappers. Heading the operation was Special Agent Alexis (Spike) Vazquez, a SWAT team veteran who had been with the Bureau since 1987. He knew this mission would be the ultimate test — one the team couldn't afford to fail.

At the request of the FBI, the owners drew a diagram of the property and the interior of the house so SWAT team members could get familiar with its layout. In the back parking lot of the Miami FBI office, agents put duct tape on the ground to outline the house and its rooms based on the owners' diagram. Then Vazquez had his men rehearse over and over how they would enter the front and back of the house and where each member would go in different scenarios.

Vazquez knew that a successful rescue operation required timing and smooth traffic flow. In a hostage situation, his men needed to get into the house as fast as possible so that the suspects wouldn't have time to react. He wanted each room commandeered by at least two agents.

Tension was building throughout the day. The lives of a mother and two innocent children were at stake. Vazquez was concerned about things that he had little control over, so his mind was flooded with thoughts: *What if the kidnappers try to leave with the family? What if a car shows up with more suspects? What if the children aren't there? What if the kidnappers are heavily armed? What if they are vicious crimi-nals who have no regard for human life? Anything can happen. We have to prepare for all possibilities.*

After hours of preparation, Vazquez and two SWAT teams of eight men each gathered in a pre-staging area at a local school a half mile away from the house and waited for authority to launch the rescue. It came at about 9:30 P.M. — almost exactly five days after the abductions. The teams drove in the darkness to the location, quietly exited the vehicles, and stacked up in the front and rear entries of the house, which had several lights on inside.

Vazquez led the front entry team while Special Agent Art Wells led the rear team. Wielding a breaching device, a leverage tool designed to crack open the front door, Vazquez's men were going to rush the bedrooms while Wells's men were responsible for the kitchen and living room. Wells's team carried a flash bang, a non-lethal stun grenade that produces a bright light and loud noise designed to temporar-ily disorient the enemy. He planned to detonate it to distract the kidnappers' attention at the rear while Vazquez and his men breached the front door.

Vazquez didn't want to throw a flash bang in the bed-rooms or bathrooms out of concern that it might hurt the children if they were in one of those rooms. He wanted speed and what the SWAT teams refer to as "violence of action" — the gaining and maintaining of physical and psychological domination in close quarters.

THE CASE OF THE ARAGAO ABDUCTIONS

"We don't know how many subjects are in there or how many weapons they have," he told his men. "We don't know exactly where Christine and the kids are being kept or even if they are in the house. We don't know how the kidnappers will react. Desperate men do desperate things. Once you go through the door, be ready for anything, be flexible, and maintain discipline. We have one chance to do this right."

His men had heard it all before. They were mostly seasoned veterans who liked and trusted one another, practiced together, and even played softball together. "Spike, we got it," a team member assured him.

But as many missions as they had carried out, this was the first time they were faced with trying to rescue a family from dangerous kidnappers. Vazquez looked each man in the eye and saw that everyone was ready to go.

While the SWAT teams were poised for the assault and rescue, Lewis and other agents set up a perimeter around the house. It was raining, but Lewis ignored it. What he couldn't ignore were the butterflies fluttering around in his stomach — the same anxious feeling he had in college before a big basketball game. *Put your trust in the SWAT team, and they'll complete their mission*, he told himself.

With the teams stacked eight men deep in front of the doors, each member squeezed the guy's shoulder in front of him as a signal he was ready. Each clutched an MP-5, a 9-mm submachine gun, with his fingers off the trigger but ready to shoot.

"Stand by, stand by," Vazquez whispered through his headpiece. "Five . . . four . . . three . . . two . . . one . . . Execute! Execute! Execute!"

His men attempted to open the door with the breacher, but the door didn't bust open right away. Vazquez didn't hesitate. Although their timing was thrown off by a couple of seconds, he shouted in his headpiece to the team in the rear, "Art! Go! Go! Go!"

The front door finally gave way, and Vazquez and his men charged into the rooms, shouting, "FBI! Don't move! Don't move! Don't move!" They needed to dominate the house before the bad guys had a chance to react.

The two agents who rushed into the first bedroom yelled, "Clear!" which meant it was empty. "Clear!" shouted the men in the second bedroom.

Vazquez was in the hallway leading to the bedrooms where a SWAT team member shouted, "I've got a subject!" Lying on the floor with an agent kneeling on top of him was Pedro Caraballo-Martinez, 20, who had been yanked off the couch. "Put your hands on your head!" the agent ordered him.

"Team One, have you seen the victims?" Vazquez asked.

After kicking open a bathroom door, another agent announced, "I found the victims! They're alive! They're safe!"

"I have a subject!" yelled an agent from the bathroom where he had collared Ewin Martinez. "Coming out!"

Within seconds it was all over. The SWAT teams had cuffed Martinez and Caraballo-Martinez, and rescued Christine, Junior, and baby Alex.

When the victims were led out past Vazquez, he noticed they were totally shell-shocked — eyes wide, faces pale. They looked stunned now that their nightmare was over. Junior and baby Alex appeared slightly injured, and Christine's face was bruised, battered, and swollen. The sight made the agent boiling mad. *What kind of cowards would do that to a mother?*

He called for medical assistance. Paramedic units that had been standing by down the street arrived within seconds.

As Christine was being loaded into the ambulance, Lewis went up to her to offer comfort. Seeing his FBI insignia, she said, "What took you so long?"

To Lewis and his colleagues, it had been five gut-wrenching days of tension and drama. To Christine and her sons, it had been five horrifying days of pain and suffering. The agent realized that for the victims, the days of captivity felt much longer than they did for the authorities trying to find them.

Alceu was at FBI headquarters when he received the news of the rescue and rushed to the hospital where he was reunited with his family. Agents arrested Ferreira, who, along with Martinez and Caraballo-Martinez, was now facing life in prison on federal kidnapping charges.

THE CASE OF THE ARAGAO ABDUCTIONS

After questioning Christine, Junior, and the abductors, the agents were able to piece together the shocking crime:

For six months, Martinez, who was the ringleader, and the others plotted to kidnap Alceu Aragao and torture him into revealing all his bank-account numbers and passwords so they could steal his sizeable assets. Then they planned to kill him.

Ferreira confessed that he befriended the Aragaos solely to gain their trust and access to their cars. He kept notes of the family's comings and goings. He casually pumped the unsuspecting Junior for information about his parents, so the culprits could select the best time for the kidnapping. On the night of the crime, Ferreira acted as a lookout while Martinez, Caraballo-Martinez, and another accomplice hid in the parking garage, waiting to pounce on Alceu the moment he arrived home from the Christmas party.

After Alceu's Porsche pulled into its parking spot, Christine and her two sons got out. Surprised that Alceu wasn't in the car, Martinez made the snap decision to kidnap them instead. As Christine held baby Alex, the three men brutally attacked her. She screamed and tried to protect Alex but dropped him after she was repeatedly struck in the face and shot several times with a Taser. Junior tried to flee but was felled when he was Tasered in the back of the head and neck. After Ferreira got the keys to the family's Lincoln Navigator, Christine was dragged away from the Porsche and shoved into the SUV. So were Junior and the baby, who were both hurt, but not as seriously as their mother. Crunched on the floor in the back of the vehicle, Christine screamed while one of the abductors held her down with his foot pressed to her back. Junior begged his mom to keep quiet so she wouldn't anger their captors.

After a 15-minute ride, Christine, who was blindfolded, was brought to a house where she was tied to a lawn chair in a closet. Left in the dark figuratively and literally, she feared for her life and even more so for her children's. She heard Alex whimpering and the voices of several people, including Junior, in other rooms. Like her, Junior was tied to a lawn chair but in a different closet.

Eventually, one of her attackers untied her and removed the blindfold. For the first time, Christine got a good look at him. She later identified him as Martinez. He told her he had been hired by the Brazilian Mafia to kill the entire family and send the Mafia a photo of all the bodies. He said he had been tailing the family for months and realized what really good people they were. Although he was a hit man, he couldn't bring himself to kill her and the children. He claimed he didn't want any money; he just wanted to help. It was all a lie — a ploy to capture Alceu and Juliana.

Christine didn't know whether or not to believe him. He seemed disoriented and flustered because he had abducted her and the children and didn't know how to treat or care for them.

THE CASE OF THE ARAGAO ABDUCTIONS

Christine was in physical agony. Her face was bleeding, her left eye was swollen shut, and her right arm was paralyzed from being Tasered. Martinez let her see her children. First he ushered her into the room where Junior was being held. Mother and son hugged and cried. Refusing to let Christine stay with the boy, Martinez took her to another room and let her feed baby Alex.

Martinez promised her that she and the kids would live. He said she just needed to get Alceu and Juliana to meet them in a safe place so he could fake the death photos for the Brazilian Mafia. "Then this will end," he promised.

Over the next four days, Martinez made Christine call Alceu 13 times on her cell phone. Making sure the conversations were kept under a half minute, he told her what to say. Seeing how unstable he was, she had no choice but to go along with his directives. Because she hadn't been given any food or pain medication for days, Christine sometimes sounded confused and dazed on the phone.

She didn't know where she was being kept — only that it was a dirty house. Loud Christmas music played constantly, often drowning out the voices of other people she never did see. One of the voices sounded like a young woman.

On Friday night, when she was wondering if she would ever get out of this alive, the SWAT teams burst into the house. Hearing the flash bang, Martinez hustled Christine and the boys into the master bathroom and warned, "It's the Mafia! They've come to kill you!"

Suddenly, an agent kicked in the bathroom door, prompting Christine to scream, thinking she and her children were about to be murdered. "We're the SWAT team with the FBI," the agent announced. "Christine, we're here to save you and the boys."

After the rescue, the sleep-deprived Lewis, who had been up for 36 hours straight, looked forward to a relaxing holiday meal with his family. On his way home, he pictured how happy the Aragaos were now that they were finally back together. A smile spread across his face and he thought, *The FBI could not have given them a better Christmas present.*

The case was far from over. The FBI had to prepare for trial as well as find two accomplices. Through their continuing investigation and a lucky break, the agents nabbed the two — Edgar Torrealba, 22, and his sister, Adda, 19, both Venezuelan immigrants.

On June 2, 2000, Martinez, Caraballo-Martinez, and Ferreira were convicted in federal district court of hostage taking. They were later sentenced to life in federal prison. Edgar and Adda were convicted for their roles in the kidnapping and sentenced to 23 years and 16 years, respectively.

The Aragaos went on with their lives — but not in their penthouse apartment. They moved to a different residence in the Miami area. Junior overcame the emotional scars from the crime and did an internship at the FBI when he was 18 before gaining an appointment to the United States Military Academy at West Point. Alex was too young to remember anything about the abduction. Christine underwent more than a dozen operations to repair the damage to her face from the beating she suffered during the abduction. Juliana became an accomplished artist living in the Miami area, while Alceu continued to run his highly successful businesses.

The family had formed such a close bond with Special Agent Jim Lewis that they get together at least once a year to celebrate their good fortune. For Lewis, it was the case of a lifetime. He said he will never forget the feeling he had when the jury came back with guilty verdicts for the three kidnappers: "It was like hitting the game-winning basket for the championship."

THE CASE OF THE
FATHER-SON SPY TEAM

Something was fishy about Harold James "Jim" Nicholson, but the FBI didn't know what.

Nicholson — the highest-ranking CIA officer ever to be convicted of spying — was securely locked away in federal prison, serving a lengthy sentence for espionage against his own country. He was under the watchful eye of the CIA and FBI, and all his communication with the outside world was monitored. His outgoing phone calls — he wasn't allowed to receive any — were recorded. Any letter that he wrote was copied at the prison and sent to the CIA for approval before it could be mailed. And any letter sent to him first had to be reviewed.

The security measures were necessary because as a globe-trotting, risk-taking spy, Nicholson had been good at his craft. Working under the cover of a diplomat for the U.S. State Department, he specialized in recruiting Russian operatives to switch sides and spy for the Americans. Nicholson, who held a "Top Secret" security clearance and wore tailored suits and expensive watches, was an agency star no matter where he was assigned — Manila, the Philippines; Bangkok, Thailand; Tokyo, Japan; Bucharest, Romania; Kuala Lumpur, Malaysia.

But in 1995, Nicholson, then 45, flunked a routine polygraph exam at CIA headquarters in Langley, Virginia, triggering a joint investigation by the FBI and CIA. The probe uncovered startling evidence. Beginning in 1994 and for the next two years, Jim had been secretly meeting with officials of the Russian spy agency SVR in Malaysia, India, Indonesia, Switzerland, and Singapore. He had pocketed $300,000 by giving up classified files, including the identities of CIA trainees, some of whom he had taught himself.

The 16-year CIA veteran was arrested in 1996. Nicholson, whose betrayal forced the CIA to cancel sensitive operations and yank highly trained spies out of the field, was convicted of espionage the following year. He was given a 23-year, 7-month sentence and sent to the Federal Correctional Institution in Sheridan, Oregon, near where his three children and parents lived.

Jim Nicholson appeared to be making the best of a bad situation by getting involved in the prison ministry and leading prayers and bible studies. But the FBI began to believe he hadn't fully given up his treasonous ways after evidence surfaced that a manuscript he wrote had been smuggled out of prison.

Now here it was the summer of 2007. Based on information provided by former cellmates, the FBI suspected Jim and his 23-year-old son, Nathan, were up to no good. So the Bureau launched an investigation headed by Supervisory Special Agent Jared Garth, of the FBI's Portland division, whose team included Special Agents Scott Jensen and John Cooney. Although they initially focused on Nathan, they never lost sight of their primary suspect — Jim Nicholson.

A background check showed that Nathan had received a medical discharge from the army after suffering a back injury during Ranger training. Living in a modest apartment in Eugene, Oregon, Nathan was a pizza deliveryman who took drafting courses at the local community college and played video games in his free time. He regularly visited his father in prison once every two weeks.

After getting approval from the secretive Foreign Intelligence Surveillance Court, which issues warrants in spy cases, Garth and his team began a covert operation to learn what, if anything, the Nicholsons were plotting. In October 2007, while Nathan was out of town, agents searched his apartment and copied his computer hard drive and various papers. They examined his bank account. They also checked his travel records, which showed that he had made two brief trips to Mexico City, one in July and one in the previous December. His email and cell phone were monitored.

The agents reviewed letters between father and son, and also listened to recordings of past phone calls that Jim had made to Nathan. One in particular that took place the previous October intrigued the FBI:

"Hey, Pa," said Nathan, answering his cell phone. "I'm on the road right now, heading back."

"Did everything go okay?" Jim asked.

"Oh, yeah. Everything went real well. Got sales for about 5K [$5,000]. And I'm even thinking of making a trip over to Mexico, come December."

"Is that right? So business is picking up, huh?"

"It sure is."

"Oh, excellent, excellent. Well, I'm glad to hear that, son. I'm really glad."

Garth and his team were convinced that Nathan and his dad had been talking in code and pretending the money had come from Nathan's commission as an insurance salesman. But the Bureau's investigation revealed that Nathan had failed at this job after only a few weeks. *There's no way he earned that money from sales*, Garth thought.

Twice that fall, agents searched Nathan's Chevy Cavalier, and in December planted a GPS tracking device on his car — all without his knowledge. While they were still testing the device, it showed that the car was parked at Portland International Airport on the morning of December 10. Not knowing where Nathan had gone, agents scrambled to figure out his travel itinerary. After reviewing his latest cell phone call, the FBI learned he had called his girlfriend at 3 A.M. to tell her good-bye.

Jensen and another agent rushed to the airport and flashed their credentials at clerks at the ticket counters, asking if any of their manifests showed a passenger named Nathan Nicholson. The agents learned that Nathan had boarded an early-morning flight on Continental Airlines for Lima, Peru, connecting through Houston. According to his reservation, he planned to return to Portland, by way of Houston, in three days.

Garth and Cooney then flew to George Bush Intercontinental Airport in Houston to await Nathan's arrival from Lima. The agents had arranged for two U.S. Customs and Border Protection (CBP) officers to pull Nathan out of a line of arriving passengers from international flights for a routine secondary search.

The FBI agents watched from behind a two-way mirror as the CBP officers questioned him about the purpose of his trip. He claimed that he had gone to Lima to scout for a place to propose to his girlfriend. During part of the search, Garth put on a CBP badge and pretended to be a supervisor, walking back and forth as he listened in. He noticed that Nathan appeared nervous and stressed out.

When the officers went through his backpack, they pulled out a PlayStation case stuffed with $4,000. They also found an additional $3,100 on him. When asked to explain why he was carrying more than $7,000 in cash, Nathan replied that he had maxed out his credit cards and needed the money for travel. The items that drew the most attention were taken out of his wallet and backpack — business cards covered in handwritten notes and a 160-page pocket notebook full of cryptic notations.

An officer took them to Garth and Cooney, who were out of Nathan's view. As the agents thumbed through the notebook, they discovered he had been dealing with the Russians for some time. Among the notations were the address of the Russian consulate in Lima; instructions about his meeting there; Nathan's code name, Dick; questions that the Russians wanted Nathan to relay to Jim to answer; instructions — including a secret signal and pass phrase — for Nathan to say at the next scheduled meeting with the Russians in Nicosia, Cyprus, on December 10, 2008; and a secret Mexican Yahoo! account and password that Nathan was to use to confirm the Cyprus meeting. Also scribbled in the pages were instructions in the event Jim left prison: "If Dad gets out, get passport ASAP. Travel to country near Russia. Up to him (Dad) (i.e. Finland). . . . Have him go to Visa section of Embassy (Friends)."

Although the mysterious notes provided clues that Nathan was involved in a conspiracy, Garth, a former prosecutor, didn't think there was enough evidence to hold the young man. The agents quickly photocopied the notebook and returned it just in time for Nathan to catch his flight to Portland.

Based on the unexplained cash and the notebook, Garth and Cooney were convinced that Nathan was collecting money from the Russians on behalf of his father. *Jim has been in prison for ten years, so what information could he possibly be giving the Russians that would be of value?* Garth wondered. *Is the money a thank-you for the years he helped the Russians?*

The FBI's intelligence experts speculated that the Russians were hoping Jim's answers might help them find a possible traitor in their ranks or at least find ways to improve their spy operations.

Meanwhile, Agent Scott Jensen was reviewing all the letters that Jim had written and was continuing to write to family and friends. Jensen noticed references that began to make more sense based on what the FBI investigation had uncovered so far. For example, Jim mentioned Lima as a nice place for Nathan to visit. This reference now made sense to Jensen, given Nathan's recent trip to Lima. In another letter, he wrote that Nathan might like Cyprus, an island country in the Mediterranean Sea. Jensen knew that was a reference to the upcoming meeting in Cyprus.

The letters were giving the FBI clues that Jim was directing Nathan to connect with Russian spies. Jim was sending him encouraging letters, often quoting lines from the Old Testament like this from Jeremiah: "Before you were born,

I set you apart and anointed you as my spokesman to the world." On Nathan's birthday, Jim wrote him, "You have been brave enough to step into this new unseen world that is sometimes dangerous, but always fascinating. God leads us on our greatest adventures. Keep looking through your new eyes."

But most of the communication between father and son occurred when Nathan visited his dad in prison.

The FBI kept Nathan under surveillance and continued to monitor the Mexican Yahoo! account that was mentioned in Nathan's notebook. In May 2008, agents spotted a message sent by Nathan that referenced the instructions found in his notebook. The subject line in the email was *"Hola*, Nancy." In part, the message read, "It looks like I will still be able to go on that vacation!" The FBI interpreted that to mean that Nathan was planning to meet the Russians in Nicosia, Cyprus.

In October 2008, Nathan sent out another email on the same account: *"Hola*, Nancy! It is great to receive your message! I love you, too. I hope to see you soon! The best regards from my brother Eugene! Love, Dick."

To Garth and his team, that could mean only one thing: The meeting was on.

Days before he was scheduled to leave for Cyprus, Nathan visited his father. An undercover agent sat in the prison visiting room eavesdropping on their conversation, which, in coded talk, included references to the upcoming meeting.

THE CASE OF THE FATHER-SON SPY TEAM

United States agents in Cyprus tailed Nathan once he arrived. They were in place with video and listening devices ready to record him and his Russian contact in downtown Nicosia on the evening of December 10.

Wearing a khaki baseball cap and holding a backpack, Nathan walked out of the Hilton Hotel. Acting as though he might be followed (which, of course, he was), he ducked down alleyways and cobblestone streets and doubled back until he arrived at T.G.I. Friday's. For nearly an hour, he stood on the sidewalk in front of the restaurant as he clutched a map and repeatedly glanced at his watch.

At exactly 7 P.M., a short, stout, gray-haired man wearing horn-rimmed glasses and a black trench coat walked up to him and asked in English, "Can you show me the way to the federal post office?"

Nathan held up the map and said, "It should be around here somewhere. Let me show you the way."

It was obvious to the agents that the two were trading coded dialogue meant to confirm each person's reason for being there. The man and Nathan strolled to a dark blue sedan parked nearby. They got in and rode twenty minutes to the underground parking garage of the Russian embassy.

Agents identified the man as Vasily Fedotov, a retired Russian spymaster who was head of counterintelligence when he was stationed at the Soviet embassy in Washington, D.C. He had posed such a threat to national security in 1986 that the U.S. kicked him out of the country. What was a former high-ranking Russian spy doing with a low-level rookie like Nathan? The FBI intended to find out.

After a series of flights to reach Oregon, Nathan arrived home in Eugene shortly before dawn on December 15. At 1 P.M., Garth and Cooney knocked on his apartment door. When he opened it, they introduced themselves and said they wanted to ask him some questions about an ongoing investigation.

Nathan was friendly, although a bit uneasy as he let them in. He offered them a drink, which they declined, and then dragged two kitchen barstools into the living room for them while he plopped down on the couch.

Cooney asked him, "Do you love your country?"

"Of course," Nathan replied.

"And would you be willing to help our country in any way you could?"

"Yes, certainly."

"That's good to hear." Cooney then went over Nathan's background with him, saying the FBI knew he had been in the army, had attended college, and had no criminal record. After some general questions, the agent asked him about his travels to Mexico City, Lima, and Nicosia.

Nathan said he went to Mexico City to check out the local architecture, flew to Lima to scout places to propose to his girlfriend, and went to Cyprus to meet up with his "battle buddies."

Cooney was a certified polygraph examiner, not that it mattered in this conversation. Based on the evidence the FBI had already gathered, he and Garth knew that Nathan was lying. But they let him keep talking rather than immediately confront him with his falsehoods, in the hope that he would give up some useful information.

About 90 minutes into the interview, Cooney thought, *He's realizing his cover story isn't working well.* The agent looked Nathan in the eyes and said, "It's time we have a serious discussion about telling the truth."

"But I am telling the truth," Nathan insisted.

"Here's the problem: What you're telling us about your overseas trips doesn't match up with what we already know," said Cooney.

Nathan's friendly mood suddenly vanished. "I haven't done anything illegal," he claimed.

Cooney reminded him, "Lying to a federal agent is a federal offense." The agent leaned forward and said, "Do you know what a mulligan is in golf? It's a do-over, taking another shot without penalty after a bad shot. When it comes to the truth, you've whiffed on too many of our questions. Nathan, we're offering you a one-time-only mulligan. Here's your chance to start over and tell us the truth."

After a brief hesitation, Nathan took the mulligan. For the next several hours, he opened up, confessing how he had become a spy messenger for his father. Nathan confirmed much of what the FBI already knew about the Nicholsons, but more important, he painted a bigger picture of what the Bureau didn't know.

He told the agents it all began during a prison visit with his dad in the summer of 2006. For months, Nathan had complained that he; his older brother, Jeremi; and sister, Star, were tens of thousands of dollars in debt, saddled with car payments, student loans, and ballooning credit-card balances. With an understanding ear, Jim whispered that he had thought of a way to ease their financial woes. He said his "old friends" in Russia might be willing to come up with some big money. Jim believed that because he was in prison for helping the Russian spy network, it was only right that the Russians help out his grown kids in their time of need. Of course, for this to happen, Nathan would have to do something "dangerous but not illegal," Jim told his son. Jim explained that he would slip messages to Nathan, who then would deliver them to the Russians.

Nathan, who idolized his dad, readily agreed to enter the spy world. Whatever concerns he had about the scheme were blunted by his blind devotion to his father. If his dad said there was nothing illegal about it, then that was good enough for Nathan.

However, the conspiracy required that father and son break prison rules against visitors exchanging notes, letters, and packages with inmates in the visiting room. So for weeks, the two practiced sneaking fake messages out from under the guards' noses and past security cameras. Nathan would buy snacks from the vending machine for his dad and put napkins on the chair next to Jim. As they ate and used the napkins, they would crumple them up until there was a little pile of trash. Near the end of their visit, Jim would sneakily drop a few balled-up or neatly folded pieces of paper in the mound of used napkins. Nathan would then pick up the pile and walk into the restroom, where he would pull out the notes, stuff them in his pocket, shoe, or sock, and toss the rest of the trash away. They were never caught during their practice attempts.

That fall, Nathan smuggled out of prison two notes that Jim had written to the Russians. The first introduced Nathan as his son and provided personal information about his family. Accompanying it was a picture taken with his son in the visiting room's designated photo area. Jim hoped it would help convince the Russians to trust Nathan. The second note asked for money.

Nathan drove all night on the 530-mile trip to San Francisco, California, where he met with an official at the Russian consulate. Despite the notes and the photo that Nathan had given him, the official was suspicious and gave the young man the cold shoulder. Nathan was told to come back in two weeks, which he did. This time he was greeted warmly by the same official, who then handed over $5,000 in $100 bills in a brown paper bag. Saying it was no longer safe to meet in the United States, he told Nathan to go to the

Russian embassy in Mexico City in six weeks to meet a new contact.

On his car ride back to Eugene, Nathan received a call on his cell phone from Jim, wondering how the San Francisco meeting went. That's when Nathan, in code, mentioned that he "got sales for about 5K."

In December 2006, Nathan flew to Mexico City and met with an older Russian he knew only as George. (George was really Vasily Fedotov, the former Russian spymaster.) Nathan handed him two new notes that Jim had scribbled on paper napkins. One of the notes said that Jim would answer any questions if the Russians would help his children financially.

George led Nathan into a soundproof room and said the Russians were interested in learning more about Jim's 1996 capture. Among the questions: When did Jim suspect he was under suspicion? What were the names of the agents who had interrogated him? What was the name of the CIA polygraph examiner?

Nathan dutifully jotted everything down in a pocket notebook. George suggested that Nathan write in code, but Nathan declined. They agreed to meet at the embassy in seven months, in July 2007. Then George opened a package on his desk and shook out $10,000 in American one-hundred-dollar bills, making sure he didn't leave his fingerprints on them. Nathan scooped up the money and left.

THE CASE OF THE FATHER-SON SPY TEAM

During his next prison visit to see his dad, Nathan relayed the Russian's questions, having first copied them from his notebook onto his arm and wrist and covering them with a long sleeve shirt. On follow-up visits, Nathan smuggled out Jim's answers on crunched-up paper.

Nathan returned to Mexico in July 2007 and gave George the responses from Jim. In the notes, Jim revealed the polygraph examiner's name, described the agents who questioned him during his arrest, and mentioned the existence of secret tunnels between two countries. In exchange for the information, Nathan received $10,000 in cash and agreed to meet George at the Russian embassy in Lima in December.

When he arrived in Lima, Nathan handed over more revealing secrets that his father had penned on smuggled notes. The young man collected another $10,000 from George, who said they should meet in Nicosia, Cyprus, in December of 2008. Then Nathan flew home, via a connecting flight through Houston, where he had a rather unpleasant search from U.S. Customs and Border Protection agents.

Having made a total of $35,000 from the Russians, Nathan shared the bounty with his cash-strapped brother and sister. He told them the money came from their grandparents' successful craft sales.

The following year at his meeting with George in Nicosia, Nathan handed over a six-page letter that Jim had mailed him from prison detailing Jim's health and family history.

After receiving $12,000 in American one-hundred-dollar bills, Nathan agreed to meet George a year later in Bratislava, Slovakia. Then Nathan flew home, where he was confronted by the FBI.

When Nathan finished telling his story to Garth and Cooney, he apologized for lying to them earlier. At the agents' urging, he wrote out and signed a confession.

"Are you going to arrest me?" he asked Garth.

"Not tonight," the agent replied.

"Really, I didn't think I was doing anything wrong," said Nathan. "I just wanted to help my dad and my family."

"It's important to understand who your dad is in order for you to understand what you did," Cooney told him. "Your father is a manipulative person, and trained to be that way. He manipulated you for his own purposes." Seeing the thunderstruck look on Nathan's face, Cooney told himself, *I'm not sure Nathan had ever thought about that before, but he sure is thinking about it now.*

FBI agents then executed a search warrant, taking his pocket notebook and laptop as well as the cash from the Nicosia trip that he had stashed in his bedroom end table.

While Nathan was confessing to Cooney and Garth, the FBI was conducting simultaneous interviews with his siblings and other family members — including Jim.

When the FBI's Scott Jensen sat down in a special prison room to question Jim, the agent slid a colorful postcard across the table. It said "Greetings from Cyprus."

The former spy stared at it for a long time without saying a word.

"Any idea why Nathan was in Cyprus?" Jensen asked him.

"My son travels a lot," Jim replied. "He went there to visit his battle buddies."

Jensen shook his head and said, "We know all about Nathan's travels, and why he went to Cyprus." Jensen then pulled out a copy of Jim's six-page letter that Nathan had given to the Russians. "So tell me, Jim, why would you have written this letter to your son about basic family information that he already knew?"

"I wanted to create a record for posterity, a family history up to this point of time," Jim answered.

"That makes no sense," Jensen said. "You wrote this letter to Nathan, but clearly it was intended for the Russians. You'd need their help if you went to Russia after you got out of prison, so you provided them with health and other information about you and your children. You wrote about your kids' financial problems because you want the Russians to help them out.

"Nathan gave this letter to the Russians when he went to Cyprus. He would never have taken on this assignment on his own. Maybe it's time you cowboy up and do the right thing on behalf of your son and come clean."

"If you're accusing my son and me of committing a crime, then I want a lawyer," Jim said, effectively ending the interview.

THE CASE OF THE FATHER-SON SPY TEAM

When the FBI told prison officials about the plot, the former spy was put in solitary confinement — where he was kept alone 23 hours a day — and was forbidden from communicating in any way with Nathan. Jim would not get to see his son for more than two years.

On January 29, 2009, the government charged Jim and Nathan with several counts of acting as agents of a foreign power, laundering money, and conspiracy. Garth and other agents arrested Nathan in his apartment, handcuffed him, and booked him into Multnomah County Jail.

As Nathan was being processed, Garth took him aside and said, "Your dad is not the hero you think he is. He sold out his country to the Russians for money. He's the one who got you into this mess. It's time you realized that and become your own man. It's time for you to grow up." Nathan broke down and cried.

Nathan eventually pleaded guilty and cooperated with the government, helping prosecutors with their case against his father. But on the day Jim's trial was scheduled to begin, Jim pleaded guilty to betraying his country a second time.

The FBI had successfully crushed the father-son spy conspiracy.

At his sentencing in December 2010, Nathan stood before U.S. District Judge Anna J. Brown and said, "Your Honor, I'm deeply sorry that this ever happened. I'm terribly embar-rassed." The judge sentenced him to five years of probation and ordered him to perform 100 hours of community service to Veterans Affairs. Given a second chance, Nathan enrolled at Oregon State University, where he studied sustainable engineering.

In January 2011, 60-year-old Jim Nicholson faced Judge Brown, who let him address the court before she sentenced him. "Your Honor, in my life I have been through several coups, I have been through a revolution, and I have been through a war," he said. "I have been marked for assassination by a foreign terrorist organization. I have been hunted by armed gunmen in East Asia, and I have been imprisoned in this country. I have gone through a heart-wrenching divorce and custody battle. But the worst day of my life was the day I learned that my young son had been arrested and charged with acts for which I am responsible."

He apologized to his children, his parents, and even the Russians — but failed to mention the United States or show any remorse for the harm he did to his country.

Judge Brown sentenced him to eight additional years in prison. Jim was eventually transferred to a federal maximum-security prison (known as a supermax) in Florence, Colorado, which houses America's most dangerous criminals.

ABOUT THE AUTHOR

Allan Zullo is the author of more than 100 nonfiction books on subjects ranging from sports and the supernatural to history and animals.

He has introduced Scholastic readers to the Ten True Tales series, gripping stories of extraordinary persons — many of them young people — who have met the challenges of dangerous, sometimes life-threatening, situations. Among the books in the series are *Crime Scene Investigators, Heroes of 9/11, World War II Heroes, War Heroes: Voices from Iraq,* and *Battle Heroes: Voices from Afghanistan.* In addition, he has authored four books about the real-life experiences of young people during the Holocaust — *Survivors: True Stories of Children in the Holocaust, Heroes of the Holocaust: True Stories of Rescues by Teens, Escape: Children of the Holocaust,* and *We Fought Back: Teen Resisters of the Holocaust.*

Allan, the grandfather of five and the father of two grown daughters, lives with his wife, Kathryn, on a mountain near Asheville, North Carolina. To learn more about the author, visit his website at www.allanzullo.com.